WHAT IS YOUR QUEST?

What Is Your Quest?

FROM ADVENTURE GAMES
TO INTERACTIVE BOOKS

Anastasia Salter

UNIVERSITY OF IOWA PRESS
Iowa City

have to help you?
nder Zale, world famous ringmaster.
how I can get out of here?
now, good luck with getting rescued.

Library of Congress Cataloging-in-Publication Data
Salter, Anastasia
What is your quest? : from adventure games to interactive
books / Anastasia Salter.
pages   cm
Includes bibliographical references and index.
ISBN 978-1-60938-275-9 (pbk), ISBN 978-1-60938-298-8 (ebk)
1. Video games—Social aspects.   2. Computer games—
Social aspects.   3. Interactive multimedia—Social aspects.
4. Storytelling.   I. Title.
GV1469.34.S52S336   2014
794.8—dc23   2014010226

CONTENTS

Special thanks to Roberta Williams, Tim Schafer, Jane Jensen, Al Lowe, and Ron Gilbert for making games that tell great stories. Without growing up on games like *King's Quest, Monkey Island, Day of the Tentacle, Gabriel Knight,* and *Leisure Suit Larry,* I'd no doubt be studying something entirely different.

This project grew from ideas formed with the advice and support of Stuart Moulthrop. Colleagues and mentors at the University of Baltimore, University of Maryland, Georgetown University, Hollins University, and beyond have all provided inspiration and support throughout this project: to name only a few, thanks to Matthew Kirschenbaum, John Murray, Nancy Kaplan, Bridget Blodgett, Kathryn Summers, Deb Kohl, Michael Macovski, Nick Montfort, Amanda Visconti, Jason Rhody, Bryan Alexander, Amanda Cockrell, and Robin Rudd. At the University of Iowa Press, I'm grateful to Catherine Cocks for her editorial guidance and her continual support of the project.

I've benefited from opportunities to present preliminary arguments from this project at various conferences: the Electronic Literature Organization, Popular Culture Association, Children's Literature Association, Modern Language Association, Connections Wargaming Conference, and WisCon 32. Some sections of this book were previously published in earlier versions: parts of chapters 2 and 5 appeared as "'Once More a Kingly Quest': Fan Games and the Classic Adventure Genre" in *Transformative Works and Cultures Journal* 2; parts of chapter 3 appeared as "Quest for Love: Playing the Women of King's Quest" in *Well Played* 1.4; and chapter 6 appeared as "Adventurers Turned Tale-Tellers: The Emergence of an On-line Folk Art Community" in *Rhizomes* 21.

Reimagining Books

Princess Nell lived in that castle and ruled over that island for the rest of her days, and every morning she would go for a walk in the garden where Harv had fallen. She had many adventures and became a great Queen, and in time she met and married a Prince, and had many children, and lived happily ever after.

"What's an adventure?" Nell said.

The word was written across the page. Then both pages filled with moving pictures of glorious things: girls in armor fighting dragons with swords, and girls riding white unicorns through the forest, and girls swinging from vines, swimming in the blue ocean, piloting rocket ships through space. Nell spent a long time looking at all of the pictures, and after a while all of the girls began to look like older versions of herself. (Stephenson 98)

NELL HOLDS AN APPARENTLY ORDINARY book and watches as its pages fill with images just for her. It talks to her and tells her stories. It answers her questions about the world, offering her adventures. Sometimes, the book comes to life, offering Nell games and challenges as she learns fighting from her stuffed animals–turned–characters. Nell lives in the world of Neal Stephenson's cyberpunk novel *The Diamond Age: Or, a Young Lady's Illustrated Primer* (1995, print), and is the owner of the Young Lady's Illustrated Primer, a "magical book" that adapts to the child reader, filling her world with lively characters who understand the things she needs to know and respond accordingly. Though the Primer is described as a book, we would better recognize it as a game, the evolved form of "edutainment" with roots in many different media. Edutainment—the combination of educational goals with an entertaining format, such as a video game—is a false binary collapsed into one genre. For those of us who grew up with computers in the classroom, the term conjures memories of *Oregon Trail* (1971, HP 2100 Minicomputer) and its simulation of the risks of nineteenth-century American westward expansion, complete with the ability to name party members after classmates and watch them virtually fall victim to dysentery and starvation. This type of narrative and historically situated game, and the genre of edutainment it helped to spawn, holds the first inklings of the forms at the foundation of the Primer.

Now imagine another child—she's holding a thin silver device with a screen, no bigger than a composition book. It reads aloud from Dr. Seuss until she focuses in on a picture of a tree, and presses on it until the screen highlights the corresponding text and reads her the word. She switches to another book, and short animations from *Toy Story Read-Along* (2010, iPad) play as she flips the pages, then opens a game and directs falling army men by moving the screen from side to side. This child has an iPad, a tablet computer with a touch-only interface first released by Apple in 2010. Apple marketed the device much like a protoprimer, and the image of the child learner with tablet in hand has already created a huge demand for "interactive" picture books and games. Different media on the iPad exist side by side, the interface and experience of one blending into the next. This child may carry her expectations of a touch-responsive interface to other media she encounters, and will be raised on stories that respond to her interests and actions.

Cyberpunk and science fiction works have continually been predicting our next narrative forms—consider the similarity between the Kinect, Microsoft's "natural" interface solution for controlling a computer with body movements, and the gesture interfaces of *Minority Report* (2002, film) and *Iron Man* (2008, film) or the holodeck of *Star Trek: The Next Generation* (1987, film) next to the promise of virtual reality. Fiction can look ahead to when the technologies that offer narrative potential today have matured and been accepted as equal to the media we already consume every day. The stories suited to new media technology, whether they are on the computer screen or a holodeck virtual reality projection room such as envisioned on *Star Trek*, have existed well before the technologies themselves. Stories have often left the reader to choose, as in the classic case of Frank Stockton's "The Lady or the Tiger?" (1882) wherein the reader is left wondering which of two possible endings is "final." In that case, the reader is given no closure, as the reader cannot input his or her decision into the story to find out what happens or learn the right answer. Stockton's story is a very simple case, while more postmodern works present many possibilities in juxtaposition for reader interaction. But Neal Stephenson's vision of the Primer seems particularly prescient for its vision not just of the advancement of one medium but of the threading of pieces of performance, book, film, and game together in a single responsive device. Brooks Landon describes it as the "ultimate electronic text, a kind of pedagogical Turing machine that by itself provides a nearly complete interactive education." But while the Turing machine evokes the theoretical limits of computational power, the Primer—and its modern counterparts—relies on responsiveness generated by storytellers.

The iPad and similar tablets and emerging mobile devices, like the fictional Primer, lend themselves to what Henry Jenkins calls "media convergence." He defines *convergence* as depending upon the intermingling of media content and forms, but not solely the media devices themselves—"convergence occurs within the brains of individual consumers and through their social interactions with others" (Jenkins, *Convergence Culture* 3). As devices optimized for the consumption of content of all media forms, they place books, games, and films on the same playing field, accessed through the same interface. The touch screen acts as a chameleon, imitating on-screen controls, keyboards, and even the flipping of a page as appropriate to the content. The convergence of media forms alongside the relative transparency and adaptability of the touch screen interface became a core part of Apple's initial iPad campaign emphasizing the device's magic. But the magic of the iPad is drawing upon a history of convergence in digital storytelling that has evolved alongside computing itself, as new tools and models for interactive narrative and the increased accessibility of those tools have allowed for a broad range of storytellers to build on these emerging models for literary interaction. Bryan Alexander describes such work as the "networked book," suggesting a strong dependence on linking both within and without (127). Nell's Primer is an apt example, particularly in its reliance upon an outside human to provide the emotional depth for the interaction—literally, a speaker for the dialogue.

For Nell and the child with the iPad, the devices in their hands appear magical. But their magic is human-generated. For Nell, the true responsiveness of the device requires a human storyteller as voice. The Primer relies on a "ractor": an actor tasked with providing voice and body for the Primer's electronic text. The iPad relies on storytellers who are, through the creation of interactive narratives, able to stay in dialogue with their readers through the mediation of apps. Defining interactivity within digital spaces is difficult because of the wide range of levels of responsiveness. Marie-Laure Ryan offers us a definition based on reciprocal dialogue: "a genuinely interactive system involves not only choice—dolls, toy trucks, and ergodic print texts also lend themselves to multiple uses—but also a two-sided effort that creates a feedback loop" (35). "Ergodic literature" is defined by Espen Aarseth as literature that requires "nontrivial effort" to "traverse" (*Cybertext* 1–2). For instance, the physical act of flipping pages to follow a linear book is a trivial effort: the exploration of a text with many choices is "ergodic," or interactive. Ryan further breaks down interactivity in digital narratives into layers based on the level of responsiveness of the system to the user. It is this space—the territory between the traditional printed book and the genuinely "interactive" book—on which I focus: a space between book and game, where the needs of storytelling are balanced with the desire (and technical ability) to create a dialogue between story, reader, and author. I argue that this space of convergence of book and game is where the distinction between reader, player, and author is narrowing. I focus on the evolution of the adventure game as a genre from its golden age in the 1990s to its current resurgence. The fans of these story-driven "ergodic" texts worked both to preserve the genre and to assert their own power as storytellers, crafting a participatory model that is spreading through the industry.

ADVENTURE GAMES

Long before the iPad, and even as Neal Stephenson was imagining his Primer, one genre of games stood in the as-yet-uncharted space between game and book. This genre was labeled "adventure games": an adventure game involves a player seeing a story through from beginning to end, following the experience of a viewpoint character—the player's avatar—on a quest shaped by the world and story crafted by the designer. Progress is inhibited not by enemies to be fought but by puzzles to be solved, whether those puzzles involve sneaking past guards, finding a key, or finishing tasks for a character in order to learn a vital clue, just as Nell gradually explores the stories of the Primer through manipulating objects and text with her own words.

The adventure game is usually mentioned as at most a footnote within gaming histories: the genre had faded from the mainstream radar and belongs to a formative past when game creators were just beginning to explore their boundaries and possibilities rather than to a modern era of games. Steven Kent's *The Ultimate History of Video Games: From Pong to Pokemon and Beyond* (2001) mentions the original *Adventure* and *Myst* (Cyan 1993), but ignores the rest of the genre. Tristan Donovan's *Replay: The History of Video Games* (2010) discusses several classics, but notes that the genre then faded into obscurity. Perhaps in part due to the seeming absence of adventure games from the mainstream, the importance of the adventure game in studying the concept of games in general has been minimized. When examining adventure games near the pinnacle of their mainstream success, Aarseth noted the challenge they presented for academic study: "Compared to all other literary formats, including hypertext novels, the adventure game's textual structure is an alien, too far removed from the genus of hegemonic literature to be recognized by any but a few xenophiles. . . . No wonder their chosen strategy most often is one of seeking similarity, bridging the gap, and trying to find a perspective, however narrow, that demonstrates that the species does not lack all the important marks of literature that we know and love so well" (*Cybertext* 109). As Aarseth's work was published in 1997, he observed this "alien" form just as it was being pronounced as dead.

Yet as the adventure game genre is being reborn—both as such and through other forms of interactive storytelling, including many iterations on the iPad—its evolution offers a model for understanding the broader future of narrative, as its structures have moved outward to reshape models of the book. I agree with Aarseth that to apply the expectations of the literary to the genre and its heirs is inappropriate; however, literature is not monolithic, and the book is far from an unchanging or constant reference. The adventure game exists alongside a number of experimental forms, some burdened with the label of "book," others with the label of "game," but in all cases both of these terms fall short. Bryan Alexander's suggested term "networked book" helps bridge this gap, but also perhaps unfairly implies that there exists a *prior* book that was not networked, an assumption that many of the works under study here would challenge. A story's association with a particular medium (or platform) does not inherently determine its interactivity. As Nick Montfort and Ian Bogost set out to define in their platform studies series, a platform in digital media can be understood as "the computing systems, both hardware and software, that developers and users depend upon for artistic, literary, gaming, and other creative development" (vii). The book is also a platform, and today is equally reliant upon changing hardware and software systems that change the potential creative output of writers and readers, as Matthew Kirschenbaum's ongoing study of word processors further illuminates (Schuessler).

Placing these different platforms in a chronological and evolutionary space illuminates the new structures upon which their narratives rely. This process of transformation in the structure of narrative by the proliferation of platforms recalls but does not precisely echo Jay David Bolter and Richard Grusin's concept of remediation, or the process by which so-called new media are constructed in part by drawing upon previous media (4). Bolter and Grusin suggest that every medium depends on remediation, and "a medium in our culture can never operate in isolation, because it must enter into relationships of respect and rivalry with other media" (65). The adventure game and its heirs can be probed with the lens of remediation but must also be understood as providing new models for narrative play.

Several elements of the adventure game make it an essential case study for looking at specific structures for interactive storytelling:

1. The focus on character rather than player makes the game "about" someone with specific gender and class traits—which the player may or may not share—and places the player in dialogue with the storyteller's world and characters.

2. The use of traditional narrative techniques interspersed with inter-

activity weds the acts of reading and playing and the forms of book and game.

3. The genre's eventual "death" and rebirth have been tied to the actions of fans as storytellers, empowering the player-creator in shaping the future of interactive narrative.

4. The modern adventure game is a powerful platform for personal storytelling, making it a viable choice for single-authored works with literary aspirations.

In unwinding the history of interactive storytelling, I reject or restructure many binaries, including the distinction between reader and player. Drawing clear distinctions between games and other media, such as books and film, was at first essential to appreciating what video games can do that other media do not so readily offer, which is interactivity. However, the desire to divorce play from seemingly passive experiences like reading can lead one to overlook the hybrid roles in between. For instance, Jesper Juul set out a strong binary between reader and player: "The relations between reader/story and player/game are completely different—the player inhabits a twilight zone where he/she is both an empirical subject outside the game *and* undertakes a role inside the game" (Juul, "Games Telling Stories?"). He appeared to discourage the literal projection of film and literary models onto games, recalling Aarseth's warning that the structures of the adventure game cannot easily be understood through the lens of traditional literary studies.

However, interactive storytelling—through the adventure game genre and its heirs among the new "magical books"—casts the reader as player, player as reader, and even player as creator in shifting interactions borrowed from several media genres. We can begin to see how the games work by examining the nature of reading practices. George Landow advances a model for the reader of hypertext that is not dissimilar to the act of reading any text: "Since readers always, but particularly in this environment, fabricate their own structures, sequences, and meanings, they have surprisingly little trouble reading a story or reading for a story. . . . This active reader-author inevitably has more in common with the bard who constructed meaning and narrative from fragments provided by someone else, by another author or by many other authors"

(197). If reading is active to begin with, it is not as different from game-play as some would argue. Ergodic texts are not limited to the digital. Adventure games can help us generate more useful understandings of the relationship between reader and player than the existing binaries. In this moment of media and platform convergence, new models for understanding our interactions with the many platforms now available must emerge, as the commonly accepted distinction between reading and play is not capable of describing the range of possible interactions we may have with increasingly "ergodic" and interactive narratives.

Ultimately, the impacts of the formal shift can be seen in every genre of narrative, not just in the adaptation of video game narratives or text room chat to shape "traditional" novels or the corresponding adaptation of books to games, but in the restructuring of those stories. Placing current texts on a spectrum between book and game requires considering interactivity. Traditional measures of narrative (or the expectations we bring to the literary canon) are insufficient when considering storytelling that takes alternative forms, as the story moves away from linearity in its overarching structure. However, a simple construction of the book as "passive" and the game as "interactive" ignores the range within the space. The printed book might appear final, but the reader's engagement with it has never been passive. In online spaces, the activeness of the reader comes to life in everything from writing and art to Tumblr sites dedicated to characters—and this is only a visible, community-oriented output of the same type of engagement print demanded before the introduction of digital technology. As Alberto Manguel chronicles in his *History of Reading*: "it is the reader who reads the sense; it is the reader who grants or recognizes in an object, place or event a certain possible readability; it is the reader who must attribute meaning to a system of signs, and then decipher it" (7). Both reader and player create meaning from the world: the dialogue of book or game is incomplete without them, and the same can be said of the hybrid forms in between.

Thus the story that is being told in today's "magical books" begins much earlier, with the first forays into digital forms of interactive storytelling on early personal computers (PCs). Text-based interactive fiction, or story worlds responsive to certain verbs and constructed with objects for a player to explore through words, took the first steps. The

introduction of graphics into the same model gradually integrated multimedia into the form, giving birth to the adventure game genre. The
rise and fall of the adventure game genre in the mainstream, its sub-
sequent life in fan production and personal storytelling, and eventually
its reemergence as a prominent form in the landscape of convergent
storytelling offer a model for understanding the range of interactions
now being integrated into our everyday consumption of narratives.

OVERVIEW

I begin by examining the adventure game's roots in other forms of
interactive narrative that owe a strong debt to text. In chapter 1, I look
at various hybrid forms existing between book and game that predate
the digital, including *Dungeons & Dragons* tabletop role-playing games
and the *Choose Your Own Adventure* gamebooks. These forms parallel
the rise of interactive fiction, perhaps the most booklike of early digital
narratives. But while these works are apparently booklike in nature, I
further examine how these forms rely not on print but on orality, offering a preview of the role communal storytelling will play throughout the
emergence of interactive storytelling.

In chapter 2, I revisit one of Nell's first questions to the Primer, "What
is an adventure?" I trace the early roots of graphical adventure games,
beginning with Roberta Williams's *Mystery House* (1980) through
the golden age of releases dominated by two companies, Sierra and
LucasArts. These early games evolved both the interface and potential
interactions within the genre. I take a closer look at one of the best-known
adventure game series of all time, *King's Quest* (1984–1998), in chapter
3, with particular attention to its position between traditions of orality,
print, and film and its construction of player-character relationships.

As the *King's Quest* series vanished, so too did the adventure game
apparently decline as a mainstream commercial form. But the epitaphs
for the genre were premature, as the story moves into the hands of fans
and new storytellers inspired by the genre's affordances. In chapter 4, I
examine the movement of creativity to the collaborative spaces of fans
in the wake of commercial disinterest. In chapter 5, I examine how

fans built new platforms for both reimagining classic adventure games and building their own entries into existing stories, which parallels the growing awareness of fan creativity and transformative works around the web. But these creators also took the genre to new spaces, and in chapter 6 I examine some exemplars of original works emerging out of online adventure game communities.

With fan-created models for creativity infusing continued life and growth into the original structures of the adventure game, it is perhaps unsurprising that the commercial game industry would eventually return to the genre. The tools of this resurgence, which I critique in chapter 7, were borrowed from crowd-sourced and collaborative models and relied heavily on the active involvement of fans. Not coincidentally, this rebirth coincided with the emergence of the iPad and other personal, touch-based devices for the consumption of media, which proved to be well suited to the heirs of the adventure game. In chapter 8, we come full circle and return to many of the forms explored throughout: gamebooks, interactive fiction, adventure games, and electronic literature. I explore the consequences of this convergence for the future of "magical books" as electronic literature built by participatory communities becomes a more prominent form of storytelling.

CHAPTER 1

Early Digital Narratives

NO GENRE CAN BE considered in a vacuum, particularly when the convergence of media is involved. I begin by positioning the adventure game as an heir to earlier forms of both digital and nondigital interactive narratives, some of which resemble the traditional printed book far more than the "magical books" previously discussed. Examining the predigital roots of interactive narrative offers an opportunity to consider the changing nature of text, particularly as some of the first games as books (and books as games) hit the market. I trace three stages of these early interactive narratives: structured collective oral storytelling (*Dungeons & Dragons*); gamebooks and *Choose Your Own Adventure* stories; and interactive fiction and text-based games.

With each variant on interactive storytelling, there is not only a tension between game and book but also a tension between orality and literacy. The well-worn cliché of the storyteller around the campfire clearly demonstrates the participatory nature of early storytelling, as listeners could chime in and together reinvent a story around a familiar framework. Walter Ong's seminal study *Orality and Literacy* chronicled the difference between the isolation of print and the immediacy of orality: "the spoken word proceeds from the human interior and manifests human beings to one another as conscious interiors, as persons, the spoken word forms human beings into close-knit groups . . . the members of the audience normally become a unity, with themselves and with the speaker" (73). Certainly, the many versions of tales born from the oral storytelling tradition bear the mark of individual and collective reimaginings—just follow the history of any fairy tale across national borders and to its inevitable reinterpretation in a Disney studio or retold with a sardonic twist in *The Rocky & Bullwinkle Show*'s "Fractured Fairy Tales" (1959–1964, television) feature.

In some ways, the printing press and its descendants are among the least participatory of narrative forms, inviting no immediate feedback and allowing only those with access to the press and distribution methods to participate fully in the production of narrative. Ong noted that the very form of print brought with it the "linearly plotted lengthy story line," with the text as the final version—"for print is comfortable only with finality . . . the text does not accommodate changes (erasures, insertions) so readily as do written texts" (130). This finality might be an illusion, as the story is transformed through the hands of the reader. The reader interprets, reimagines, and even rewrites through adaptation, parody, or the creation of fan works. The digital networks that have followed in the wake of print promise to restore immediacy of connection between reader and writer, re-creating the "campfire" on a global scale. But more important, they have erased the finality of print and challenge the image of the printed book as unchanging or lacking the potential for interactivity and dialogue after the type is set. This apparent favoring of orality is echoed in Marshall McLuhan's examination of the impact of the electronic platform on the written word: "electric technology seems to favor the inclusive and participational spoken word over the specialist written word" (*Understanding Media* 82). While McLuhan—writing in the 1960s—was reacting to television and radio, his words seem particularly prescient given the role of the participatory oral tradition in shaping the examples to follow.

PLAYING STORIES AROUND THE KITCHEN TABLE

Even during the emergence of computer platforms, interactive storytelling thrived in models not too far removed from the campfire. The *Dungeons & Dragons* (1974, print) system was invented to provide a structure for the telling of group stories run by one person, the Dungeon Master (Gygax and Sutherland). The Dungeon Master is as much a player as the rest of the group, and the players always have the ability to defy the Dungeon Master's narrative and rewrite the story. Collective storytelling in a *Dungeons & Dragons* game appears to the outsider as a group of people talking around a table, illustrating their words with simple props in the form of game manuals and sheets and sheets of paper describing monsters, characters, items, and environments within the game. Otherwise, the stories and worlds exist only in the imagination of the players. As a role-playing game, *Dungeons & Dragons* relies on the players serving as actors in a rules-based drama with narrative merging from action. Each player takes on a character that exists in no real form other than as a list of attributes, abilities, and equipment, which the player creates according to the rules in the manual and embodies based on his or her own vision of the character's personality. *Dungeons & Dragons*, which is still played today even with the countless multimedia options for interactive fantasy, suggests that the idea of group storytelling continues to hold an appeal that flashy graphics and complicated interfaces need not necessarily replace. *Dungeons & Dragons* offers a model where complex fantasy can be modeled systematically based on rules established in the manual, with the modules provided heavily focused on medieval high-fantasy and combat. A video role-playing game, in contrast, provides a specific visual world with particular characters to interact with following a set of rules. The game cannot deal with any interactions it is not programmed to handle, unlike a Dungeon Master.

The relationship between *Dungeons & Dragons* and traditional books was clear, as players bought the print manual guides to the worlds and rule-sets—a model also seen in other tabletop role-playing game systems that followed, including the more flexible *Generic Universal Role-Playing System* (*GURPS*) published by Steve Jackson Games in 1986, which substituted the more general "game master" for "Dungeon Master." The game worlds also spawned novels, including large series that last to this day. Of these, one of the most notable is the *Dragonlance* series, which began with the *Chronicles* trilogy (1984, print). When the trilogy was re-released in an annotated edition, it included side notes that offered insight into the game sessions that brought the characters to life. The text owes its characters in part to the players. As Tracy Hickman observed in his annotation to the text:

> We played the first module of the *Dragonlance* series as I was writing it, occasionally convening in our apartment after work. . . . My friend, Terry Phillips, took the Raistlin character—only roughly defined at that time. When I first turned to him to ask him a question, he answered me in

character—with a rasping, whispered voice filled with cynicism. . . . Raistlin as we know him today, was born. (Weis and Hickman 24)

The *Dragonlance* novels exist both as complete stories and as game modules waiting for players to take their own journey through the same conflict. The best play sessions are thoroughly cocreative, with players building from a Dungeon Master's vision with the same unexpected consequences as Terry Phillips's portrayal of Raistlin that night—a mage haunted by a dark heart and a tense relationship with a strong and handsome twin brother overshadowing him. While Terry Phillips is not credited on the novel's cover, and he is not acknowledged as an "author" of the text, would the world of *Dragonlance* have been the same without his contribution? Consider Raistlin's legacy—another trilogy, the Legends series, and two prequels known as the Raistlin Chronicles written entirely to satisfy fans of the complexity of this one dark character. This set of results from game play recalls Ong's model of the "audience" and "speaker" as united in storytelling, a relationship very different from that of the final printed book and the presumed (if not actually) passive audience as receptacle for the text (Ong 72–74). But the text novels are also more than a transcription of play: they provide motivations and perspectives from multiple characters, encompassing a more complete story than any one player experiences in *Dungeons & Dragons*.

Tracy Hickman also observed another difference between these games and the finished novels: "Novels, unlike games, require proper foundation for their characters" (14). This is a claim worth revisiting, as *Dragonlance* is far from the only example of a game-to-book transition—and vice versa, as a number of book series would move their narratives formally in the opposite direction. The differences between book and game in these cases can be particularly revealing, as the construction of story is moved from a clearly cocreative, open-ended space like Margaret Weis and Tracy Hickman's gaming nights to a single- (or in this case double-) authored, linear, and complete format. These distinctions can appear to reproduce the reader and player binary, as a player at the original gaming night helped shape the story that a reader consumes. How does this compare to the experience of a player who picks up the published *Dragonlance* modules, with the story of the novels and guidelines for the quest at their center in place? Perhaps his or her experience is found somewhere in between, with reading (the module's content and prewritten quest text) coexisting with play (the interactivity between scenes that moves the players through the quest). And certainly the book was in no way the final text in the gaming world, however complete in format—it served as a starting point for dialogue.

GAMEBOOKS

The *Choose Your Own Adventure* (hereafter *CYOA*) gamebooks first appeared in 1976 and were at their most popular during the 1980s and 1990s—not coincidentally the same time as digital narratives were taking off on the computer and video game consoles. But the books owe a debt to experiments with interactivity within the boundaries of the printed book that began even earlier. For instance, Raymond Queneau's *One Hundred Trillion Poems* (1961, print) is a kind of adult "gamebook." It consists of ten sonnets, sliced into fragments and bound in a book. The reader is supposed to "discover" or "write" his or her own new sonnet by assembling some of the strips. This method of writing poetry calls into question the authorship of the sonnets: although each individual sonnet appears to have depth of meaning, it was not itself written in the traditional mode, thus challenging the usual understanding of authorial intent. Queneau created the content, the reader has the power to arrange it, and the system determines the limits of what is possible. Thus the question of who "creates" the sonnet blurs.

This type of experimentation is typical of Oulipo, which Daniel Levin Becker described in his study on potential literature as "the laboratory in which some of modernity's most inventive, challenging, and flat-out baffling textual experiments have been undertaken" (6). By contrast, *CYOA* gamebooks offered a more limited range of possibilities. The books begin with an explanation of the genre: "This book is different from other books. You and YOU ALONE are in charge of what happens in this story" (Montgomery). But the reader's control over the story was limited to making a series of choices among those options the book presented. The narrative split into many paths throughout the pages of a printed book, so that the player's central activity was reading a section of narrative and making a choice. Upon making the choice, the player could turn to the indicated page to find the outcome. Thus *CYOA* gamebooks often incorporated several endings, although most of them were unsatisfactory. A typical example occurs in the surreal *Choose Your Own Adventure 15: House of Danger* (1982, print), in which the player takes the role of a young detective entering a house built on the site of a Civil War prison. If the reader makes the wrong choices, the detective can end up dead at the hands of ghosts, aliens, and other evildoers:

> "You refuse, do you?" shouts the creature. "Well, we have another use for humans. In fact, it is our main use for humans."
>
> With that, he takes out a small device from his pocket and aims it at the three of you. A beam of incredibly cold light—its temperature hundreds of degrees below zero—freezes you, Lis, and Ricardo into solid blocks of ice.
>
> Then the man takes out a rubber stamp from his other pocket and stamps your forehead: "HUMAN MEAT—GALACTIC PRIME/SOURCE—PLANET EARTH—GRADE A." (Montgomery 88)

All such macabre fates are followed by the words "The End," indicating not the end of the book but of the player's opportunity to make choices in the story.

While the *CYOA* gamebooks use a fairly straightforward model of decision making, other gamebooks emerged drawing upon more complex mechanics, including those of *Dungeons & Dragons*. Remember Terry Phillips, the player responsible for bringing Raistlin Majere to life in *Dragonlance*? Fittingly, his time with the character did not end with that series, and as part of the *Dungeons & Dragons* creative team he continued to write stories about Raistlin's identity. In 1985 he wrote his own entry in a series of *Advanced Dungeons & Dragons Adventure Gamebooks* called *The Soulforge*. The book offered the reader-player the chance to fill the shoes of Raistlin Majere prior to the *Dragonlance Chronicles*, as he headed for the test all mages must pass to fully reach their power. *The Soulforge* gamebook was part of the "Endless Quests" initiative from TSR, the corporate creators of *Dungeons & Dragons*, capitalizing on the similarity between the game and these choice-driven nonlinear novels. One such "Super Endless Quest Adventure Gamebook," *The Ghost Tower*, promised the reader "All the thrills of the DUNGEONS & DRAGONS game in an exciting new Gamebook!" Unlike the *CYOA* series, these gamebooks added additional mechanics, including the use of character stats and dice rolls to determine success or failure. The promise of *Dungeons & Dragons* thrills also communicated the intention of the series to function as a "solo" version of a quest-driven game, with the book rather than a Dungeon Master evaluating success or failure for each of the player's choices. Raistlin's identity card replaced the character sheet and allowed the player to grow his or her skills through play. Years later Margaret Weis would revisit this story in a new *Dragonlance* novel—also entitled *The Soulforge*, but including the authoritative account of Raistlin's test, with all decision making now in the hands of the author and character.

Like graphic adventures, books in the *CYOA* style faded for some time—the seminal *CYOA* series went out of print in 1998, only to return when relaunched in 2006 with rebranding accompanying the same familiar premise: "the interactive, multiple-choice multiple-ending series is among the most popular series for children ever published, with more than 250 million copies sold in 38 languages" (Chooseco, LLC). By this time, the original audience for the *CYOA* novels had grown up and seen the genre age with them, as smaller releases such as 2008's *You Are a Miserable Excuse for a Hero* by Bob Powers parodied the movement from the optimistic decision making of youth to the paralysis of adulthood. Others, like the "Do-Over" novels by Heather McElhatton, offered a glimpse of the broad potential of grown-up life to a teenager who had just graduated from high school by offering the reader a series of possible mistakes and a wide variety of endings. Some authors mined literary sources for inspiration, as in Emma Campbell Webster's *Lost in Austen* (2007, print), which invited the reader to step into the shoes of an Austen heroine and navigate the many possible fates for a woman in that world, while keeping track of each decision's impact on accomplishments, fortune, connections, intelligence, and confidence in an Austen-appropriate version of *Dungeons & Dragons*–style stats. And others, like Jason Shiga's *Meanwhile* (2010, comic), reinvented the form as a graphic novel. (I revisit Shiga's *Meanwhile* later, as it also became a striking example of interactive storytelling on the iPad.)

FROM *DUNGEONS & DRAGONS* TO COMPUTER GAMES

As a relatively new entry in the history of media, the tradition of interactive storytelling through the means of computer gaming technology has a short but fast-paced history. The same type of rules-based system that *Dungeons & Dragons* was based on could translate into the technical worlds emerging alongside these imagination-powered games. Players of *Dungeons & Dragons* were often the same people designing computer games in these early stages, which John Borland and Brad King describe as a time of highly independent, noncorporate creation. Players of games were at this time quickly switching roles to become creators; at this point, one programmer could master the limited available technology and build a game relatively quickly (Borland and King 41). The idea of a store dedicated to selling computer games was still rare, so games circulated among the small community of players mostly through established connections and friendships before any organized efforts to sell the works were made. While *Dungeons & Dragons* manuals could easily be integrated into the shelves of a bookstore, often housed near other hybrid forms such as graphic novels and gamebooks, computer games were still finding their space.

Tracing the origins of the modern computer game requires stepping back only a few decades to the early 1970s when the prototype for the mainstream computer system was emerging in the academic laboratories of universities across the country. The oft-cited first videogame, *Tennis for Two*, was made mostly to generate interest in the technology and not with any expectation of profit or use outside the lab (Chaplin and Ruby 36). This lack of clear corporate and monetary incentives for creating video games, which were as much a novelty as the hardware itself (which was still far too expensive to be available outside of specialist labs and industry), continued to be the norm until 1972 when Atari was formed—just as *Dungeons & Dragons* was released. Atari produced the arcade game *Pong* to place beside the familiar pinball machines of public venues and in one year saw profits of more than $1 million (Chaplin and Ruby 38). This first commercial videogame lives on despite its simplistic graphics and nonexistent storyline, perhaps in large part due to the repetitive yet addictive appeal of its gameplay. It has aged gracefully, and fans have ported it repeatedly for both PCs and mobile devices.

Pong and *Dungeons & Dragons* are the two origin points of the computer game industry most often cited (Borland and King). The dramatic contrast between them represents the two extremes typical of gaming: on the one hand, storytelling-based gaming, in which progress is slow and focused on the narrative; and on the other hand, the action and reflex-gaming—in which speedy hand-eye coordination is key to victory—of the electronic arcade game. While the arcade-based gameplay on dedicated systems would eventually give way to cartridge-based consoles with interfaces descended from the arcade joystick and button pads, storytelling games would find their way onto the PC, first in forms not so different from a *Dungeons & Dragons* game module written in text awaiting the player's cocreative input. Several early digital games even built upon the *Dungeons & Dragons* series explicitly, using the same mechanics and systems to build role-playing games that combined randomized tactical combat with exploration of fantastical worlds.

From these two very different starting points, our modern conceptions of game genres would emerge, each incorporating different blends of gameplay, environment, story, and interface. PC game genres were born out of text and systems of game mechanics relying on database structures, while console games were born out of arcades and reflex-driven, level-based games with limited controls. This distinction would prove essential to the evolution of games on the two platforms, even as new competitors such as Nintendo brought story to the console games and added morality to play. Arcade machines were the ultimate in hardwired content, with each box and interface dedicated to a single game. Consoles began similarly, but the introduction of cartridges allowed for one hardware to play multiple games—although at first these games did not appear remarkably different from one another. However, these were almost all games, with only a few breaking out to other genres with either creative tools or production- and learning-focused programs. A few experiments (like the NES keyboard peripheral) tried to bring documents or other modalities to the game consoles along with games to teach typing, but ultimately failed to capture much of a market for early computer experiences on the television. In contrast, clearly story-driven games—text-based and otherwise—were initially mostly popular on computers, where users were already growing accustomed to the idea of a convergent device with utilities for both work and play, and a keyboard allowed for verb-driven interaction.

As action games developed, Borland and King write, "Fighting and shooting games were gaining prominence in the late 1980s and early 1990s. . . . The computer game market was changing even more, as the industry's momentum swung unambiguously to the IBM PC and its clones" (81) and away from the arcade. The PC was particularly suited to gaming development, and remains the computer platform of choice. The game at the center of the movement, *Doom*, the 1993 creation of Jay Wilbur at Id Software, "would explode like a rocket shell in the collective consciousness of PC gamers, changing the way that people thought about the computer as a gaming platform" (Borland and King 89). The game started a new genre: "the 'shooter,' as *Doom* clones would come to be called, essentially took the kill-fast-or-die concept of *Space Invaders* and blew it up into a fully realized 3D world defined by its demonic creatures and blood-spattered walls" (Borland and King 89). In first-person shooter games, the player assumes the role of an avatar within the world, but that avatar is a noncharacter—usually the only important quality of this avatar is its status as a viewpoint window for the player to interact with the world. The player is the one doing the shooting, and the distancing element of controlling an avatar doing these actions is generally reduced by the fact that the player looks directly through the avatar's eyes and acts through the avatar's body. There is no further in-game development of a relationship between the player and the character.

This direct involvement of the player in the violent acts of a game is one of the common complaints of commentators on the negative impact of gaming, because it can be seen as a direct experience of killing, and perhaps have a desensitizing effect (an argument addressed by James Paul Gee in *What Video Games Have to Teach Us About Learning and Literacy*, who identifies the positive impacts of even violent games). An argument of this sort assumes that this avatar identification is seamless, and that the player is acting in a virtual world in a manner that might impact actions within real life. However, these games do rely on the presence of a stereotyped role that the character generally fills: in *Doom*, the avatar may have no specific character, but he is positioned as a space marine fighting for survival. This patterning remains part of the player's experience—it is acceptable in the player's world to act in an indiscriminately violent manner because that is what the situation calls for, and success by the rules of the game is only possible by mastering the mechanics and reaching the game's endpoint.

The most direct descendants of the *Dungeons & Dragons* gameplay are role-playing games. These are based around a character battling to the conclusion of a quest, such as saving a kingdom or finding a magical artifact. Both the role-playing game genre and the adventure game genre are driven by story: the game progresses through narrative events moving toward a goal or conclusion. The adventure game genre emerged around the same time as the other genres, and it incorporated elements of the puzzle game along with a personalized focus around a character's quest. However, for a game to be defined as an adventure game and for the genre to be distinct from others, combat cannot be the focus. The intense experience of the first-person shooter games and the hybrid experience of the role-playing game would stand in sharp contrast to the more sedate and cerebral playing experience of the adventure game. In both adventure and role-playing games, a player has an embodiment on the screen in the form of the playable avatar, a virtually embodied representation generally directly controlled by the player. In the essay "Playing at Being: Psychoanalysis and the Avatar," Bob Rehak studies the distinction between the positioning of the spectator and the player. An avatar in a video game is a "direct extension" of the player: "The video game avatar, presented as a human player's double, merges spectatorship and participation in ways that fundamentally transform both activities" (Rehak 103). Spectatorship through the avatar is a dual experience: the player can be watching the progress of his or her avatar on the screen, or looking directly through the eyes of the avatar, as in a first-person shooter. The correspondence of the player's physical body to the on-screen avatar is not necessarily a simple extension of the senses: "Players experience games through the exclusive intermediary of another—the avatar—the 'eyes,' 'ears,' and 'body' of which are components of a complex technological and psychological apparatus. Just as one unproblematically equates a glove with the hand inside it, we should not presume the subjectivity produced by video games or other implementations of VR [virtual reality] to transparently correspond to, and thus substitute for, the player's own" (Rehak 104). In contrast the act of typing, the main mode of interaction in early adventure games, bears little resemblance to the actions of an avatar in those games. In the context of adventure gaming, avatars are figures on the screen that "move around, pick up, put down and manipulate objects, talk to each other, and gesture . . . under the control of an individual player" (Farmer par. 8).

The central difference between role-playing and adventure games is in the specificity of the avatar body being inhabited. In a role-playing game, the player has choices that typically encompass not only the name and appearance of the character but also the class. Class in a role-playing game usually follows fantasy archetypes—mage, thief, warrior, priest, or other variations. The player can take on any one of these archetypes and make this created character the center of the game. In contrast, in an adventure game the player does not control the characteristics of the avatar; the story of the game is specific to the programmed avatar. In an adventure game, the player might be handed Raistlin's shoes and identity to fill, with an understanding that his or her actions are to some extent scripted with Raistlin's choices and identity outside of the player's control.

As a result of these differences in the relationship between the player and the avatar, the story in a role-playing game is less grounded in the history and nature of a predetermined character and written to allow any character to be at the center. This genre cares more about the advancement of that character in power than of the development of the story: a character in a role-playing game advances in level by gaining victories in battle or in the game storyline. The avatar earns experience points by killing monsters and completing quests, and this means that the character is trying to beat the game by becoming powerful enough to overwhelm any obstacles. The character in an adventure game, on the other hand, moves forward by trying to solve puzzles in progression, each of which contributes to the storyline. Perhaps most limiting of all for game narratives, the role-playing game storyline has to accommodate multiple characters that the player creates: it is a generic story. In the adventure game, the player inhabits a specific character who undergoes a personal experience. The player advances not through completing quests, but through achieving the goals of the character as dictated by the overarching narrative.

Early PC text-based games included both role-playing and adventure games, both finding their start in the first narrative "dungeon-crawler." Five years after *Dungeons & Dragons* had made its mark, William Crowther created a text-only game entitled *Colossal Cave Adventure* (1975, PDP-10 computer), which offered a text-based world for the player to explore in the same manner as a spelunker navigating unfamiliar caves. The title would be shortened over time to simply *Adventure* (1976, UNIX/IBM-PC). Another programmer, Don Woods, revamped the title and incorporated puzzles with the traditional exploration model, one of many instances of collaboration after-the-fact providing a model for improving and extending games. Espen Aarseth notes that the story of *Adventure* is often misattributed or misdated, perhaps in part because it provided "a paradigm of collaborative authorship on the Net: one person gets an idea, writes a program, releases it (with the source code); somewhere else another person picks it up, improves it, adds new ideas, and re-releases it" (*Cybertext* 99). The accessibility and portability of *Adventure* are distinct to PC games (as opposed to console and arcade games) and shaped the type of games that emerged in this genre.

This simple text-only game was the first adventure game and achieved eventual widespread popularity through ports to the early PCs of the time. In a text-only game, there are no graphics—everything is described in text. The lack of visual images of the world means that these gaps are left to be filled in by the player, a concept that would mostly disappear from gaming with the fall of text-based games by the wayside but was already familiar to players of *Dungeons & Dragons*. Interactions with the world occur through verb commands. For instance, a character in a text-only game moves as a result of the typed commands "go north," or similarly phrased commands, then takes in the environment through the typed command "look." The parser can only interpret a limited set of commands, but this vocabulary allows the player to address the world, and the player's words become part of the game. A printed record of gameplay would include both the player's actions and path intertwined with the scripted elements built into the environmental narrative—in short, a story.

The close connection between text and PC games reflects in part a constraint of the original hardware, which began with text-based operating systems and command interfaces. PCs also provided the tools both for the creation of software and the playing of games, which is part of what enabled *Colossal Cave Adventure*—the original text labyrinth, with the phrase "You are in a maze of twisty little passages, all alike" surviving as emblematic to this day—to take its own journey in the hands of fellow PC users who, using the same interfaces, ported, extended, and built upon its foundation (Crowther). The adventure game genre—text and graphic—owes both its name and its continual extensibility to *Colossal Cave Adventure*'s model.

And now it will come full circle back to the world of text with the successful funding of a Kickstarter campaign for making a physical board game from *Colossal Cave Adventure*. (Kickstarter offers a model for crowd-sourced funding that I revisit later.) The board game project, launched by Arthur O'Dwyer, notes that the original game "has been considered (for whatever reason) to be in the public domain," thus inviting reimaginings like this one (O'Dwyer). This assumption is common in the cocreative history of game adaptations, but particularly so with text-based games in which all the "assets" are so easily deconstructed and reimagined. Thus text-based games particularly lend themselves to this form of adaptation. Like text itself, they are easily edited by a single person, and thus easy to remake and spread even in the limited storage environments of early PCs. Furthermore, the lack of graphics means that artistic changes to the world are easy to make, as transforming the words themselves can change the impact of the game on a player's imagination. The same foundation of a playable gamespace can readily switch genres or meanings with a change in text—unlike graphical games, which are not so readily adapted to new purposes.

INTERACTIVE FICTION

Text-based games experienced their own brief era of popularity as a number of games inspired by *Adventure*'s framework were released, including a direct spiritual successor, *Zork* (Apple II, Commodore 64), which, although still offering worlds rendered only through text descriptions and the imagination of the viewer, was commercially successful by the standards of the new industry in 1979. These games were grouped in a category that would come to be called "interactive fiction," primarily published by Infocom. The genre of interactive fiction refers to the traditional story feeling of much of the text-only game experience: the player takes actions that reveal more and more of a story. Nick Montfort defines the interactive fiction genre in his study *Twisty Little Passages*. He notes three characteristics of interactive fiction: the use of interaction to reveal the world and move the story forward, the parallel to games in having an "optical outcome" for the player to try and reach, and the use of a computer program to handle input and output (Montfort 13–14). The focus on text alone gives the interactive fiction genre, not burdened with the label of "game" or the expectations thereof, a more obviously literary pattern where the player is actively writing and reading, often in stories with clearly inevitable endings. Interactive fiction still survives today in independent programming efforts in part because the format offers the basic potential to take stories and turn them into playable environments. Infocom's games had so much in common with gamebooks that several of their titles were converted to the form: *Zork* gamebooks were sold as "What-do-I-do-now" books, based on "the most popular computer game of adventure/fantasy" (Meretsky back cover). The stories followed quest novels set in the same world as the original *Zork*, using simple decision models adapted from the mechanics of their interactive fiction, but with child protagonists for the readers to identify with as they play through the story.

These playable environments did not have to be limited to the experience of a single player. Online versions of text-based games could support multiple players, all interacting with and changing the world at once, in Multi-User Dungeons (MUDs). MUDs began to emerge in

1978 in limited text-only forms, with no graphical capabilities. These games allow for a collaborative experience of the story, as Janet Murray describes: "MUDs are intensely 'evocative' environments for fantasy play that allow people to create and sustain elaborate fictional personas over long periods of time" (44). Murray could just as easily be describing a group of dedicated *Dungeons & Dragons* adventurers, since MUDs brought back the multiplayer experience typical of that game and initially not supported by computer-based interactive stories. At the same time, sustaining "fictional personas" who built a relationship with an environment was integral to text-based games such as *Zork*, in which the player's investment in the adventure was required to map the space and understand complex puzzles to make success possible. While some of these text-based worlds are still alive today, their most direct heirs in communal play are the massively multiplayer games such as *Everquest* (1999, PC), *World of Warcraft* (2004, PC), and even *Second Life* (2003, PC), which offer players the opportunity to construct an entire virtual identity during highly social play.

The golden age of text-based games is still associated with Infocom, which made no secret of its view of these games as playable novels. The term interactive fiction was the first of many apparent contradictions that would shape this emerging genre. When we picture reading as passive, that is in part a physical description. The reader's actions in most books are prescribed and repetitive: he or she turns pages. A game, on the other hand, offers choice of action, recalling Aarseth's definition of ergodic text as difficult to traverse. When a traditional codex makes similar demands, it is labeled as such. A child's activity book, or even a *CYOA* gamebook, wears its "interactive" nature—and the limits of its interactivity—on its cover. This does not mean that reading is not active before the "game" piece is involved. The actions taken while reading mostly involve mental construction, and are therefore often imperceptible to the outside viewer. Perversely, it is very common for video games to be accused of requiring no significant mental engagement precisely because so much physical activity is involved, and the mental processing involved in playing a video game does not much resemble our more contemplative ideal of the reader.

Games in the format of interactive fiction, whether single-player or multiplayer, are particularly adept at communicating the type of story experience that Jenkins calls a "spatial story," in which the player finds the story within his or her environment by taking on the role of "you." Infocom marketed its games with the promise that "you" would be in the story, rather like Disney and Universal Studios market their theme parks. Indeed, Jenkins compares environmental storytelling to an amusement park attraction ride, and for interactive fiction this is particularly apt ("Game Design"). Consider, for instance, a Disney ride such as Splash Mountain, where every aspect of the ride contributes to the atmosphere, including warning signs to turn back if afraid of heights and boats shaped like logs with seats. As riders move through the space, they read short messages grounding them in the world of Brer Rabbit so that they will be prepared for the conflict that the space holds. Like the rider of such an attraction, the player of an interactive fiction story is a visitor to a world that previously existed only within the designer's head, and through his or her interactions the visitor soaks up the atmosphere of the world while following the rules of the experience, thus functioning as a tourist abiding by the adage, "When in Rome . . ." Visitors know that they cannot steer the log vehicles off their tracks, but they can gather information about the environment and therefore gain a better sense of the story, even as they proceed through its narrative arc (and inevitable drop).

The experience of a story world of this kind was therefore both enhanced and limited when graphics became part of game environments. At the emergence of the adventure game form in the 1980s, creators adapted traditional texts. The nature of the format would seem to encourage direct adaptation, but instead the initial efforts evoked, more than they transcribed, their source materials. As Nick Montfort noted in his foundational study on the emergence of interactive fiction, "*The Hobbit* was one of the earliest commercial works of interactive fiction to be based on a book. . . . The puzzles were at times obscure and would require knowledge of the book; the major incidents in Tolkien's novel were the direct basis for the situations of the IF [interactive fiction] work. (This would turn out to be the case often in interactive fiction that was 'converted' from print fiction.)" (Montfort, *Twisty Little Passages* 171). The player often needed to know the book to progress in the game because of how much was absent in the conversion: the game did not reproduce much of the context, particularly in describing the world and characters. Usually in these conversions the actual author of the original story was not involved, one rare exception being in the making of *The Hitchhiker's Guide to the Galaxy* (Apple II, DOS), which in 1984 would become one of the most successful such adaptations: "*Hitchhiker's* was the first case in which a veteran IF author and programmer worked closely with a famous author to produce something that was almost certainly greater than what either would have devised working alone" (Montfort 174). Appropriately, the puzzles require the player to make good use of his or her towel and enjoy Vogon poetry (Adams and Meretzky). This cocreation—a seminal Infocom title—gestured toward the potential of interactive fiction when authors took a role in shaping the story worlds.

The results of further collaborations between authors and interactive fiction creators reveal another parallel between interactive fiction and a literary form. Another game from 1984 features the collaboration between creators and writer Robert Pinsky—a future poet laureate of the United States: "More than any previous work, *Mindwheel* (despite being called 'an electronic novel') revealed the profound connection between interactive fiction and, not the novel, but poetry. Most obviously, there were poems on the surface of it" (Montfort 177). The cover of *Mindwheel* even lists Pinsky as an author—a credit not often emphasized in the world of computer games. Computer games emphasize the role of designers, artists, and programmers, but the actual writing of in-game text and dialogue is usually not the product of a specialist but rather the work of someone whose primary task is one of these other roles. Montfort sees a poetry in the actions of the player using text to address challenges: "The player character of *Mindwheel* is supposed to pursue a relentless quest but cannot help assembling art during the process: filling in the blanks of poems as well as performing actions that uncover new phrases and poems, spaces and conversations" (181). *Mindwheel* opens with a surreal textual introduction that appropriately positions the player interacting with a keyboard:

You lie face up on a table in the stark laboratory. There is a hospital smell, and dozens of electrodes are attached to your body. "Are you ready to begin your journey? Or would you like a description of the situation? Or perhaps you would like me to tell you about the Minds?" asks Doctor Virgil. He waits for your reply. Suspended in front of you is a computer keyboard.

The poetic interplay of these exchanges is in the use of language, which was a crucial element in early interactive fiction but a less obvious element in later games. In these early systems, the player was literally relating to the world with words, using combinations of verbs and nouns to progress in the story (Pinsky, Hales, and Mataga). These interactions are not the complete sentences of prose but instead the loaded phrases of a poetic style. The game was appropriately bundled with a book, a novella written by Pinsky to provide context to the surreal challenges the "mind-adventurer" faced.

With the advent of graphics, it would be easy to see interactive fiction merely as a precursor to other genres emerging from its roots. But that oversimplifies, as Stuart Moulthrop reminds us in his response to the apparent minimal attention paid to hypertext and interactive fiction: the addition of new capabilities, such as graphics and sound, did not eliminate creative interest in the genre, even if it remained a "niche." It is likewise impossible to separate interactive fiction from those forms that emerged around it, for "no fan is an island," and the convergence and intersection of interactive fiction with other genres continues (Moulthrop, "For Thee"). Consequently, interactive fiction and the tools for creating it—such as Inform, a free language and compiler for creating text-based games using a descriptive language very akin to English grammar—exist alongside graphical adventure games but are often associated with a different type of user. Nevertheless, while interactive fiction works such as *The Hitchhiker's Guide to the Galaxy* were once best-selling games, nearly two decades have passed since the form has been viewed as commercially viable.

The study and creation of interactive fiction also survive as one facet of electronic literature. Electronic literature can be defined in many ways, but N. Katherine Hayles offers a valuable functional definition: "a first-generation digital object created on a computer and (usually) meant to be read on a computer" ("Electronic Literature"). This excludes the traditional eBook, adapted directly from a print object and without any particular use of the affordances the computer offers, although it is still open to fairly broad interpretation. A full history of electronic literature is impossible to do justice to here, but the Electronic Literature Organization's bibliographic overview offers further introduction (Gould). The organization also offers this evasive definition for electronic literature: "works with an important literary aspect that takes advantage of the capabilities and contexts provided by the stand-alone or networked computer" (Gould). Many early works of electronic literature are hypertextual, using web technologies and affordances (such as HTML, or "Hypertext Markup Language," and links between file nodes) as their structure. Such novels resemble gamebooks in their organization and suggest one model for the evolution of literature. This definition could be borrowed and applied to interactive fiction, adventure games, and many other convergent forms that emphasize narrative, and thus offers an important starting point for evaluating the literary influence of these interactive fictions.

For instance, the electronic literature movement has claimed Crowther's *Adventure* as an early text (Rettberg), although not everyone endorses this connection. As Noah Wardrip-Fruin's analysis of "playable media" noted, some creators of early electronic literature differentiated themselves behind the motto "this is not a game" in order to make a "distinction between mere text games and work worthy of consideration by the literary community. Between low and high culture. Between trivial play and serious writing" ("Playable Media" 214). But there is convergence and overlap between the two both in critical study and in structure, and the two can both be classified under Wardrip-Fruin's term of "playable media" ("Playable Media" 211). Playable media, when placed alongside ergodic literature and interactive narrative, emphasize the act of play while the latter two privilege the storytelling aspect of the work. However, the term also suggests by the addition of play to media that play is outside the media's initial intention and affordances.

Indeed, the history of electronic literature includes several works easily identified with interactive fiction, such as Nick Montfort's metatextual *Book and Volume* (2006, PC/Inform 6) and Adam Cadre's subversive

9:05 (1999, PC/Inform 6), which plays with the reader-player's expectations of his or her character and its goals. 9:05 generally only truly reveals its "winning condition" on a second playthrough, when the player has already learned from a first attempt that the character is a murderer (Cadre).

One particularly powerful example of this type of interactive fiction is Andrew Plotkin's *Shade* (2000, PC/Inform), which appears at first to be a puzzle game: the player has to try to escape from his or her apartment and find the tickets for a trip to the desert. As the player interacts with the room, it gradually turns to sand. The player becomes aware that he or she has already made the trip, that he or she is in the desert, that he or she has died, and that the helicopter he or she heard was looking for but never found him or her. There is no way to "win" *Shade*—the player cannot change the inevitable, and as the sequence takes hold, the more the player tries to grasp at straws in the mirage around himself or herself, the more final the compiler's reaction is, as every object turns to sand in his or her reach (Plotkin, *Shade*). If printed out, the final transcription of a session playing *Shade* would show the futility of the player's actions in a world where powerlessness must be accepted in embracing the inevitable end—a very different concept than the usual game in which winning is rewarded. In *Shade*, the only way to avoid death is not to play. Andrew Plotkin has continued to write this kind of interactive fiction, and we will revisit his stories later.

In sum, the first playable stories to reach the computer screen did not look much different than the printed page—the differences were hidden from the casual observer in the software, in the code that provided the logical structures and text parsers for the story. These works were entirely text-based and relied upon the player's use of the correct command to manipulate the world of words. But as any avid reader already knows, words are enough to convey adventure, just as Will Crowther's *Adventure* offered reader-players a crawl through caves known to Crowther from his own real-life explorations. In text-based games, the parallels between reading and play are easy to perceive. Text-based games also hold as a primary affordance the luxury of contemplation and time to read and make decisions based on a narrative context.

This is in stark contrast to the action-based, reflex-driven genres that emerged alongside text games, where the mechanics of play leave little time for decision making. The process of traversing a text-based adventure game or work of interactive fiction resembles the choice-making systems of *Dungeons & Dragons* and *CYOA* gamebooks more than the frenzy of playing *Doom*. But as graphics were added to the same foundational mechanics as interactive fiction, the first recognizable graphic adventure games would diverge.

CHAPTER 2

Adventure Games

THE ADVENTURE GAME genre's roots are interwoven from imagined stories cowritten by players around a dinner table, gamebooks with "you" as the protagonist, and worlds of interactive fiction. While the label "interactive fiction" would come to be associated primarily with the text parser and the absence of a graphical environment, the spirit of the early terminology (and the connection to gamebooks) would remain essential for defining the adventure game genre, which existed on the outskirts of the accepted definitions of gameplay. As computer games evolved the type of highly on-rails, story-centric gameplay that adventure games represented with their close tie to traditional textuality would be more and more suspect as true interactivity, and the clashing demands of narrative and agency would become more prominent as the expectations of players changed in light of fully realized and exploration-based worlds.

The challenge of creating a truly interactive narrative has been debated in the past (and in my own analysis above) as a problem of balancing the demands of narrative and play. The designer is trying to tell a story, but the more linear and unified that story becomes, the more the player is confined and imprisoned within it, left without agency in the world of the game. Too much freedom, and the player is left wandering without guidance or motivation, and the quest loses its power to motivate the player to progress through the world. As I showed in the previous chapter, the adventure game genre can be considered a descendant of interactive fiction, and is similarly characterized by the dominance of story over gameplay, often with only one "happy" ending. The game involves overcoming obstacles set on the path to reaching that conclusion.

In *On Interactive Storytelling*, Chris Crawford begins by examining the role of storytelling in games. Crawford notes that low expectations on the part of gamers often allow games to escape the actual confines of storytelling: "Games have never paid much attention to the many structural requirements imposed on stories. . . . Players don't complain when games jerk them through wild dramatic gyrations because they don't expect games to follow the protocols of storytelling" (14). This is particularly true of a game such as *Doom*, in which the vague storyline involves a Mars space marine fighting creatures for reasons that are barely elaborated upon. The plot advances around moving from level to level, but that progression is neither explained nor particularly important. The focus in *Doom* is on interacting with the game world, but only through using brute combat. Crawford defines interactivity as "a cyclic process between two or more active agents in which each agent alternately listens, thinks, and speaks" (29). Crawford's definition of interactivity describes an ideal in which the player acts and the game responds to that player's specific action. The reality of most games even today is that the active participation in this dialogue is limited: the player acts and the game responds in one of the ways that the game designer has programmed it to in anticipation of possible player actions. However, adventure games rely on a conversation that goes beyond the actions of the player within the space: the conversation between player and designer as they collaborate to tell a story.

The metaphor Crawford uses for interaction is conversation. This allows him to easily differentiate the experience of the game from an experience such as watching a movie: "Reaction, no matter how intense, is not the same as interaction. If you're watching a great movie, and your heart is pounding with excitement and your fingers trembling with emotion, you're still not interacting with the movie because it's not listening to what you are saying, nor is it thinking about anything" (Crawford 30). This definition echoes Marie-Laure Ryan's understanding of interactivity as dialogue, a back-and-forth between system and user. Just as in a conversation, the experience of interactivity always depends upon the individual involved: "millions of people can play an interactive storyworld, and each one can experience something that nobody else has ever experienced . . . it responds to each person individually" (36). This level of interactivity is dependent upon a fully realized world, one in which the player's interactions are more meaningful than simply choosing from a few dialogue options or completing quests to find an object—this idea defines a hypothetical ideal while ignoring the strengths of the game genres we already have.

In light of these definitions, adventure games might not appear to be much more interactive than *Doom*. Adventure games succeed not at the limitless interactivity of this pure definition but at the limited interactivity demanded by narrative. Stuart Moulthrop recently addressed the critical history of setting interactivity and narrative at odds: "It has become unfashionable to speak of antipathy between games and stories, after some defining schoolyard moments in which early ludologists faced down their literary harassers, winning a grudgingly respectful truce. Yet there remains a necessary and inevitable tension between these sharply different forms of fiction" (Preface xxi). While *Doom*'s interactions lack choice, adventure games provide freedom within constraints. The constraints are not arbitrary, and thus they reflect the "tension" Moulthrop noted between story and game: this is not an external tension, but an internal mechanism. However, the interactivity of adventure games is in the opportunity for responsiveness within limits: the tension between narrative and play is used to tell the story. The genre probes the real potential of interactive stories, not as massive productions, but as acts of authorship with the intimacy of oral storytelling. I will briefly examine the history of early adventure gaming alongside some of the theoretical debates over truly interactive narrative, beginning with arguably the first "graphic" adventure game, *Mystery House* (1980, Apple II), and continuing through the golden age of gaming dominated by rival houses Sierra and LucasArts. Throughout this early history, it is particularly crucial to note the role of the fans and players, who would themselves become the storytellers of future generations of adventure games, even after the genre fell out of favor in the commercial market.

HOUSES OF MYSTERY

When Roberta Williams, one-half of the partnership that would create adventure game titan Sierra On-Line, first encountered the text-based world of interactive fiction, she thought there was something missing. Her solution took the form of *Mystery House*, the first graphical adventure

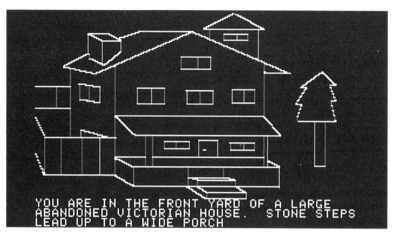

1. *Mystery House*. Sierra On-Line Systems, 1980.

game, which offered an abstracted Victorian house for the player to
explore room by room through command interactions copied from interactive fiction (Williams and Williams). The exterior of the house (fig.
1), with its limited color palette and architectural "3-D" drawing style,
demonstrates both the limitations of early graphics and the ability of the
designers to create a foreboding atmosphere in spite of them.

Mystery House launched the adventure game genre. Each new game
further integrated the words and pictures until full voice-over and
mouse interaction removed much of the text from the gameplay. But
the stories remained at the center of the games, and even the first game,
with its blocky line graphics, did not fall into the forgotten abyss of abandoned digital files. Nick Montfort's "Mystery House Taken Over" (2004,
PC/Mac/Linux, Glux) project preserved the files and substance of *Mystery House* for reinterpretation and rebirth and is a powerful example
of fan/academic intervention in and transformation of even the earliest of graphic adventures. The project included a reimplementation of
the original along with ten different transformations ranging from Guy
Minor's revenge tragedy, "Occluded Vengeance," to Michael Gentry's
surreal "[You wake up itching]."

These many versions made more than two decades after the original,
the variety of which can be seen in figure 2, are an invitation to go back

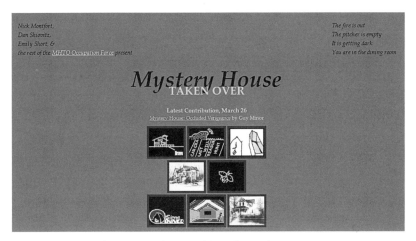

2. "Mystery House Taken Over" website. Nick Montfort et al., 2005.

into the mystery house and discover something new (Montfort, "Mystery House Taken Over"). When contrasted with the original *Mystery House*, the thumbnails for the remakes show added color, reworked themes, and even full conversions of the underlying engine. One such reworking by noted interactive fiction author Emily Short retitles the story into "Mystery House Possessed," a text-only game that describes the house in a way that the graphics of the era would never have supported: "Here, to the south, is the house. The paint has peeled off, the candy-like trimming largely fallen away, and all that is left is the structure with its narrow puritan bones plain to see. . . . A wizened tree grows before the house, most of the leaves gone, bearing out of season eight pale blue flowers."

Such remakes demonstrate the enduring potential of one of the most literary genres among games, and constitute a form of creative "modding," or retelling. Adventure game fans would regularly undertake a similar type of deconstruction and reconstruction with other games as well.

While projects like "Mystery House Taken Over" recall the early days of computer graphics, the industry's shift to graphics was gradual. Initially working within a static visual environment, players continued to input actions through a text parser and act in part as cowriters of the game's story, albeit within the limited vocabulary that the parser could translate into objects or actions. The introduction of the mouse dramatically changed that interaction, permitting clickable text buttons to replace verbs for sparking in-game actions, and eventually by using iconic representations of action choices and direct point-and-click interaction. The introduction of soundtracks and recorded dialogue voice-overs also changed the literary form of the adventure game. These elements demanded less of the player as coauthor, as reading and writing moved from a fundamental method of play to a secondary form, preserved only in games labeled throwbacks to these early genres.

THE FIRST ADVENTURES

Soon, the creator of *Mystery House* was taking graphics in adventure games to the next level. Their next epics incorporated animated visuals in the place of the static graphics of *Mystery House*, and with each generation the games gained more complexity in dynamic illustration. The era of animated adventure games brought the incorporation of graphics and the avatar to the genre. This was a radical change from the precedent set by interactive fiction, particularly in the evolution of interface. In an animated adventure game, initially the text-based commands remained, but instead of seeing only text description and a basically static image such as that of *Mystery House*, the player saw a graphical screen of the area the avatar currently occupied. At the next stage of development, the player directly manipulated the avatar. If the player typed the command "go west," the avatar on the screen went west. When mouse technology made these screens directly clickable, instead of typing the player could point to the place or object in the graphic with which he or she wanted to interact.

From these beginnings the two main publishers of classic-era 1980s and 1990s animated adventure games emerged—Sierra and LucasArts. Throughout the 1990s these and other publishers continued to release adventure games, eventually switching from the 2-D cartoon-style graphics of the early games to the 3-D graphics that had become standard throughout the industry. In 1987, Lucasfilm Games—which would soon be renamed LucasArts—released an animated adventure game entitled *Maniac Mansion* (Commodore 64, Apple II), the first to use a gaming engine LucasArts would refine for most of its adventure game releases. This gaming engine was entitled "Script Creation Utility for Maniac Mansion" (SCUMM). Designed by Aric Wilmunder and Ron Gilbert, the SCUMM gaming engine allows the easy transfer of an adventure game to multiple platforms, meaning that the game could be played on many of the different models of PCs available at the time without as much difficulty in rewriting the code. The SCUMM interface has a unique character: it places the traditional text-based verb commands for a game environment as options on a menu bar that takes up a third of the screen. This system allows the reader to choose a verb such as "Pick up" and to enact that verb on an object from the game world, such as "Pick up key." The menu options leave no need for guesswork in determining what actions are possible at any point in the game, giving the player a visual codex revealing the possible interactions with the world. By contrast, the text parser offered players an open point of entry where the limits of interactivity had to be probed to be known.

Even as these technical changes altered the game environment, adventure games continued to be story-driven. The goal is to progress through an overarching narrative by solving puzzles. The player controls a character and sees that character through a specific quest by overcoming puzzle- and story-based obstacles that range from finding a key to fit a lock to outwitting a guard at the entrance of a temple. The story-driven portion of this definition is more crucial to understanding this genre than it might be with other forms of computer games. For instance, the first-person shooter (as in the previous example of *Doom*) often functions on a story-line as simple as "kill the invading aliens" without that being problematic or limiting, whereas the expectation for adventure games is that the story will be an original experience worth revealing through the solving of puzzles: the progression of the story is in effect the reward of the game. However, adventure games cannot simply narrate a story: they somehow have to involve the user in the experience and make him or her part of the narrative development. For the player to care about the game, he or she must first identify with or be interested in the character at the center of the game. The mouse bridges some of the gap between a player's actions and a character's actions, enforcing the connection even as the third-person camera view discourages the player from adopting the character's gaze.

The user's relation with the interface is different in the adventure genre than in other genres of gaming, in part because of the close ties to the text-parser model from interactive fiction. As I pointed out in chapter 1, the emphasis on fighting in most other genres requires a playing style that is closer to the reflex-based games of the arcade than the quests and stories of *Dungeons & Dragons*. Reflex-based games also use an interface that is based on the point-and-click model, but in an action game or console interface the focus is often on speed and hand-eye coordination—speed is essential, as the environment itself is hostile. In an adventure game, the user is expected to take time to explore the environment and find the elements that make it possible to solve puzzles and advance the story. Quest solutions are not supposed to be immediately obvious but must be discovered through exploration. The text parser made this exploration feel limitless, while the mouse restricts the user to manipulating only what is visually represented. However, the text system only offered the illusion of limitlessness. In reality, the only actions possible in either system are those intended by the designer.

Another important development that proved essential to the adventure game is the integration of game saving as a mechanic. Other early genres and platforms did not require saving: the arcade game, for example, is a public machine. As a public rather than private gaming experience, particularly from its early development, the arcade machine generally does not have a "save game." Players cannot stop playing and then later pick up where they left off, or save their progress before taking a risky or uncertain action. Instead, usually arcade games are divided by levels, and finishing a level allows the player to learn a pass code to access the next level sometime later. This system emphasizes the generic nature of the experience: it does not matter how the player finishes the previous levels; the next level is the same for everyone and thus can be accessed separately from the player's own path and identity.

By contrast, the "save game" is an absolute necessity for the adventure game to exist. An adventure game user frustrated in interacting with the game environment has the option to save before taking a risk or to quit the game for a time and take a break—a temporary rather than final ending. As a result, the "save game" allows for progression of a game in more than one sitting—indeed, as Jesper Juul notes, it allows for games lasting hundreds of hours, not just a single sitting as with the arcade games (*Half-Real* 111). As an adventure game usually features a narrative that moves forward through the action, not having the ability to pick up exactly where the game was left off would make such games impossible. In this light, playing an adventure game is more like reading a book: the player picks up the book on the page where he or she left off rather than beginning at the first page every time. However, that metaphor does not fully apply. A book is always the same from start to finish. A reader might skip from chapter to chapter, or read the ending first, but these activities do not change the linearity of the original text. The only save device generally available in a book is the bookmark, which marks a point in the narrative without consideration for how the reader arrives there. In an adventure game, it is the player's specific trajectory that must be preserved to allow the finishing of the player's own story: the experience is not generic, and it is not a question of simply moving on to the next level or chapter.

EARLY AVATARS

As the introduction of graphics and the "save game" brought embodied avatars to the adventure game genre, memorable characters started to emerge, built through text, graphics, and interaction. Early avatars relied heavily on stereotypes and familiar archetypes to explore the possibilities of interactive storytelling, often carrying with them the baggage of other genres—primarily books, comics, and film. In most cases, players entering an adventure game know that at the start they will not be able to choose the characteristics of the avatars that will represent them. One of the few exceptions is *Maniac Mansion*, which offers players multiple predetermined avatars from which to choose. The game follows a familiar plotline: rescue the girl. In this case, the girl is Sandy, a cheerleader who was kidnapped by Dr. Fred Edison, the owner of the mansion. Leading a mission to rescue Sandy is her boyfriend, Dave, but the player has the choice of who accompanies Dave on this perilous task (Gilbert, *Maniac Mansion*). The available avatars in *Maniac Mansion* are teenage stereotypes. Choosing among them is not a matter of aesthetics, however, as each character has an impact on the possibilities of game-play. There are six choices from the group, of which two can be brought on the task: Syd, a musician; Michael, a photographer and the lone person of color (sadly, still notable among computer game avatars from any genre); Wendy, a writer; Bernard, a geek; Razor, another musician and the second female character choice; and Jeff, a surfer. But even though the characters are stereotyped, LucasArts used them to make fun of the stock female characters and plot typical of the ongoing *King's Quest* series, created by rival developer Sierra. In *Maniac Mansion*, the story seems to resemble that of *King's Quest II*—man goes to rescue a princess. But in *Maniac Mansion*, the princess is a cheerleader kidnapped by a mad scientist, and the man doing the rescuing is fairly incompetent at his task. The friends make the plot move forward, not the knight or the princess.

It is possible to defeat *Maniac Mansion* and rescue the cheerleader with any combination of rescuers. Of the choices, however, the most useful is a male, Bernard, pictured in plate 1 in an iconic combination of glasses and collared white shirt. The line of text below the visual image of the mansion's interior is the limited text parser for processing "sentences" or actions made from the available abilities. Bernard is a geek, capable of repairing all the electronic devices that are broken within the house—his verb "fix" is in the list of options below. His role in the first game is so pivotal that he is the lone playable avatar to return in *Maniac Mansion*'s sequel, *Day of the Tentacle*, suggesting a desire for continuity of character identification between the two games as best represented by the most versatile avatar. In this game, Bernard's *Maniac Mansion* cohorts are gone, but he does have two companions in a quest that spans three eras of time (Grossman and Schafer). Each character is trapped in a different era after the opening sequence of the game, but able to communicate through the sending of supplies flushed through the time-traveling port-a-potties. One of Bernard's companions is a woman named Laverne, a medical student with an interest in dissecting hamsters. She is portrayed as eccentric, with messy hair, unfashionable yet unique clothing, and eyes that don't match. She is for the most part no one's love interest, the exception being one tentacle who finds her attractive while she is wearing a disguise. This is an early example of progressive gender representations in adventure games by comparisons to other computer game genres, a distinction I return to when I address the *King's Quest* avatars in chapter 3.

Another example of the golden-era adventure game avatar is seen in another LucasArts game, *The Secret of Monkey Island* (1990). Throughout the series, the lead character is a classic ditz: blond hair, more beauty than brains, and big, unrealized ambitions. This character is, however, male, and he is constantly in pursuit of both his dreams of being a "mighty pirate" and the would-be love of his life, island governor Elaine Marley—a woman who is always portrayed as more successful, levelheaded, and intelligent than the male avatar, Guybrush Threepwood. Elaine Marley begins the series running for the office of governor, and throughout is shown pursuing and achieving that goal while granting Guybrush the time of day only when her own ambitions are met (Gilbert, *Secret of Monkey Island*). The player thus occupies the role of the bumbling fool, playing an avatar that no one respects. Making progress in Guybrush's quest is difficult because of his low standing in the community, and the player may find additional motivation in the continual heckling of nonplayer character bystanders. However humiliating the role, the quest for attention, and for self-transformation from social outsider to "mighty pirate," is one the player can easily identify with. These avatars and their goals are parodies of the heroic quest, set against not only other adventure games of the time but other heroic characters from media. These characteristics began to establish the adventure game avatars as human characters, rather than less relatable ideals (as best embodied in *Tomb Raider*'s Lara Croft and *Doom*'s grimacing space marine).

In another Sierra franchise set not in a distant time but instead in a relatively modern urban life, Leisure Suit Larry of the series of the same name is a badly dressed man with sex on his agenda. The player guiding him in this quest experiences the same frustration as the character when Larry fails, as he usually does, to attract the attention of any of the women who see him coming. Larry is another case of the undesirable avatar: his quest is hindered by his own inept and off-putting nature (Lowe, *Leisure Suit Larry*). The player embodying this avatar is hardly living a dream life, but instead is taking on a quest of desperation. Already, the adventure game genre avatars are positioned as something other than wish fulfillment: these avatars possess no abilities beyond that of the player. Playing this kind of avatar means taking the moral position that one's own goals and ends are more important than honesty or respect for women, but the entire experience is situated within an environment of humor and lighthearted mockery that gives these actions less meaning. Contrast this with the machismo of the first-person shooter, with Duke Nukem (1991) shouting, "It's time to kick ass and chew bubble gum. And I'm all out of gum." Notably, both Larry and Guybrush Threepwood have seen a post–golden age rebirth in commercial projects aimed across platforms, something I revisit in chapter 7.

ADVENTURE "GAMES"?

Players enter any of these adventure games with an introductory sequence that introduces them to the persona of a specific character as part of enabling a literal out-of-body experience of an entirely different life, that of the avatar. Thus a player of adventure games cannot expect to have much control over the start-up of the game, when the stage is set for the predetermined narrative. This reliance on a set of standard expectations is true of any genre: with the first-person shooter, for instance, players expect that an interface will be provided and explained to allow for navigation and shooting. With the adventure game, the required interface needs to allow for the completion of the quest. The crucial characteristic of the adventure game is the presence of the quest. It motivates progression: the avatar has a quest or objective to complete that the player assists the avatar in achieving. This narrative structure creates the expectation of a final victory: when the quest is finished, the player expects the game to come to a conclusion and reveal its meaning.

The genre of the adventure game has standards to aid the player in identifying and engaging with the quest. First, the player can interact with the environment presented on screen. These interactions take many forms, but the primary interaction is usually with nonplayer characters. Nonplayer characters are controlled by the computer; they are graphically represented in the same style as the avatar, but there is no person behind their actions. Often these characters are stationary, waiting for the player to enter the scene and activate their roles. They offer programmed responses, and usually serve as quest givers and objects of quests. The player can speak with nonplayer characters through the avatar. Sometimes the player has a choice of what to say, and in other games the dialogue is preset. This situation again offers a window into the tension between avatar and player: the player may have a choice of what to say, but those choices are determined by the avatar character's personality and situation—the player does not have absolute power. The game sometimes puts words in the player's mouth, leaving him or her bound by the system, unable to say what he or she would choose.

Second, the player can interact with objects in the environment. These interactions range from lighting a torch or flipping a light switch to collecting pieces to make a voodoo doll. In the earliest days of adventure games, quests involving objects tended to be quite simple: in one room, there is a locked door; in another room, a key. When the player comes across the key, the avatar can pick it up and place it in the inventory—a virtual space often represented by a backpack that can hold seemingly limitless amounts of virtual things. Objects in this inventory and in the larger world can be used and combined, often through interactions as simple as putting that key in the locked door. More complicated interactions are possible using the same puzzle structures in different combinations, as devices can be constructed with objects to solve puzzles—for instance, for the aforementioned voodoo doll the player might collect hair, cloth, and thread from different places, then put these objects together, one after another, to create a voodoo doll. That doll might then be used to torture a particular person and so on through a sequence of events. The options for using objects allow the player to interact with and alter the world of the game, and to thus be part of the environment itself.

The mechanics and frameworks governing the potential abilities of the character are rules taken from narrative, not from structures inherent in gameplay. Given these constructions, it is easier to see how adventure games fit under an extended definition of interactive fiction and are not necessarily best understood under the rubric of "games." In *Pause & Effect*, Mark Stephen Meadows refers to this kind of work as interactive narrative: "An 'interactive narrative' is a form of narrative that allows someone other than the author to affect, choose, or change the events of the plot" (238). The positioning of adventure games within this category depends somewhat on the design principles at work in any given game, as often an adventure game is structured along fairly set lines in a nodal progression; the difference that two different users have in playing the game is in the ordering of events, not in the events themselves. Because of this progression, some adventure games qualify as what Meadows terms an "impositional interactive narrative": "A heavily designed story, such as one of the 1980's *Choose Your Own Adventure* books . . . it guides you with strict sets of individual rules that only allow the reader a narrow margin of decisions" (63). Adventure games do commonly display elements of this definition: choices are set, and the user must follow the path or abandon the game. But as the previous discussion of the *CYOA* noted, the narrow limits of these gamebooks were imposed in part by the limits of bound codex as database for a decision-making system. Digital systems can allow for more "twisty little passages" within the story even as they also impose rules and structures.

At the other extreme are what Meadows calls "expressive games," which rely "less on the series of events and [behave]s more like architecture: The visitor is allowed to roam freely, explore, investigate, and make changes in the environment. The specifics of a narrative plot are far less defined and, as a result, the breadth of interactivity is much wider" (63). Expressive games include some of the progeny of adventure gaming and role-playing games, such as massive multiplayer online games like the early LucasArts game *Habitat* and its successors, *Everquest* and *World of Warcraft*. In these games, the idea that the user is part of a story is still present; however, what is far more important to the game-playing experience is the building of a consistent world experience.

Adventure games can fall in different spaces on the spectrum, from expressive to impositional. Lurking somewhere near the middle are adventure games such as the classic *Myst* from 1993, wherein the player explores a world with great freedom and little guidance. Certain actions would gradually reveal more of the environment and the overarching storyline. *Myst* was a success not only with habitual players of computer games but also with a wide audience, in part because people found the exploration of the environment engaging and intuitive—visual and musical cues prompt player involvement. The authors in this case were successful in creating an interactive narrative that Meadows would say creates accessibility for the reader, one of the great challenges of the genre: "The author of interactive narrative has to present all the forking paths by telescoping information and offering perspective. So the art of interactive narrative lies in the author's ability to simultaneously imagine (and illustrate) each of these views and make all of them accessible for the reader" (69). That is a challenge that textual works inherently handle differently than digital works, as the very format of the physical page constrains any notion of "forking paths," while digital space enables infinite diversions. *Myst*'s environment, as shown in plate 2, literally embodies forking paths on its twisting island as rendered in early 3-D graphics and textures.

In *Myst*, the epic scale and beautiful environments gradually tell the story, giving it a feeling of mythic significance. In games like those that LucasArts produces, the scale is less epic and more personal and the focus more comic, as with *Day of the Tentacle*'s (1993, DOS/Mac OS) highly cartoon-influenced graphics and "Purple Tentacle" villain. The constant switching of perspective between *Day of the Tentacle*'s three playable characters further requires a story that takes an omniscient view, as the narrative often demands the display of events outside the knowledge of the user's avatar, or at least outside of the knowledge of one or the other of the characters, given the spatial difference in their individual perspectives. This omniscient perspective is also reinforced by the graphical decision to place the characters controlled by the user on the screen, rather than having the screen reflect what that character sees. Adventure games can thus simultaneously draw on approaches from multiple media in their use of perspective; as Meadows notes: "Perspective is odd because it's something that exists both visually and cognitively. . . . It exists in the form of a first- and second-person perspective in literature and has visual equivalents in painting, architecture, and interface design" (162). This is another way in which the internal convergence of media influences is expressed in interactive narratives in general and adventure games in particular.

TRANSMEDIA STORYTELLING

Several early adventure games externalized this relationship with literature and other texts. I addressed this in adaptations such as the text-based games *The Hobbit* and *The Hitchhiker's Guide to the Galaxy*, discussed in chapter 1. But adaptation is only one relationship a game can have with texts: some games go beyond the existing narrative. Releases where the game experience extends the experience of an existing narrative world are examples of the "transmedia storytelling environment" as Henry Jenkins defined it, in which the story of a world is not contained in any one media product ("Game Design"). Jenkins offered the example of *Star Wars*: "The *Star Wars* game may not simply retell the story of *Star Wars* [the film], but it doesn't have to in order to enrich or expand our experience of the *Star Wars* saga. We already know the story before we even buy the game and would be frustrated if all it offered us was a regurgitation of the original film experience. Rather, the *Star Wars* game exists in dialogue with the films, conveying new narrative experiences through its creative manipulation of environmental details" ("Game Design"). These new narrative experiences can range from games centered on particular characters related to the primary *Star Wars* (film and book) canon whose stories were not part of the *Star Wars* saga to the experience of players within the massive multiplayer games *Star Wars Galaxies* (2003, Windows PC) or *Star Wars: The Old Republic* (2011, Windows PC), who shape stories by adding their own characters to the universe.

In a transmedia environment, one can experience any iteration of the story—for instance, a *Star Wars* movie or adventure game—independently, but one will discover more of the story by indulging across media platforms: "One can imagine games taking their place within a larger narrative system with story information communicated through books, film, television, comics, and other media, each doing what it does best, each a relatively autonomous experience, but the richest understanding of the story world coming to those who follow the narrative across the various channels" (Jenkins, "Game Design"). In the *Star Wars* series, the books might feature a highly developed historical saga and introduce the stories of new important characters, while flight simulator–style games such as *TIE Fighter* and *X-Wing* offer the opportunity to share the experience of a soldier in the armies in conflict throughout the films. In these cases, each medium offers a different strength: while it would be possible to write a book around the battles of a Tie Fighter pilot, the game offers the same reflex challenges as piloting and a chance to mimic the experience of the pilot through actions rather than words. Conversely, the game cannot offer the narrative complexity and depth of information provided in a novel. Through this interaction of experiences the world of *Star Wars* is fleshed out, creating the possibility for a fuller experience of the narrative through varied ways of joining the universe.

The connection between adventure games and more traditional narrative forms in transmedia storytelling universes continued even as graphics were gradually integrated into the parser-based model of interactive fiction. Reading and playing continued to be related pursuits. In 1993, *Companions of Xanth* (MS-DOS) was released by Legend Entertainment Company bundled with a physical book by Piers Anthony. The book, *Demons Don't Dream*, offers one detailed possibility for the outcome of the quests of two characters playing a computer game that transports them into the land of Xanth, a fantastical world that is in some ways an alternate Florida where almost everyone has magical powers of some sort. The book plays out a literal transformation of player into avatar, as the two protagonists gradually realize that Xanth is not a computer-generated construct but a real world (Anthony). The players enter the world of Xanth once they come to believe in it and care about the fate of its inhabitants, though they initially believe them to be only characters in a computer game. *Companions of Xanth* offers only one playable character, Dug, but includes a nonplayer character companion who accompanies the character on the quest as a guide and potential ally (Alpin par. 3). The interface system in *Companions of Xanth* uses a verb-based model and offers text descriptions that echo some of Piers Anthony's own style of description to accompany the images. In the book, many puns rely on subtleties of language, such as the similarity of sound between "pale" and "pail":

"And where may I find this magical solution?"

"It is beyond the pail."

"Beyond the pale," Dug said. "Of course."

"You must take the pail and bring the solution back in it. That is the only way."

"I shall try to do that. But just how far beyond the pale, uh pail, is this solution?" (Anthony 43)

Within the game, the humor is visual. The player encounters a pail sitting in the path, and acquires it to hold the "solution" after it is brewed through solving another puzzle. However, the emphasis on verbal humor and exchanges with characters is minimized, leaving players to sort out the puns for themselves.

Another company, Cyberdreams, published a game based on a Harlan Ellison short story written in 1967: "I Have No Mouth, and I Must Scream." Ellison was directly connected to the production, writing the story in a longer version specifically for the adventure game of the same name (1995, DOS/Mac OS). He was also the voice of the supercomputer manipulating the fates of the playable characters (Mobygames). The game was particularly unusual in that it was essentially impossible to win in any real sense, although the five victims endured some fates that were more desirable than others (Ellison, Mullich, and Sears). Staying true to Ellison's vision, the game dealt with themes of sanity and human failings in intensely psychological gameplay. As one reviewer wrote:

> Each of the characters in the game is afflicted with a distinct psychological condition (paranoia, depression, etc.) and his or her actions are affected by these tendencies. Each character's scenario is basically constructed to subject each of them [to] whatever traumatic experiences caused these afflictions and forces them to explore the nature of their humanity and find a way to deal with and overcome their fears. These forays into each character's psyche can only be described as disturbing as best, with images ranging from people impaled on meat hooks to mutilated children in a Nazi concentration camp. (Hoelscher)

These images indicate that Cyberdreams intentionally targeted an adult audience with the game; for the images to exercise their full power, players must understand them and have a strong reaction to them. For a child, these images would mainly serve to horrify. For an adult, they facilitate an exploration of darkness in the human psyche.

As part of a growing landscape of transmedia storytelling, adventure games suggest an expanded definition of interactive narrative. The juxtaposition of the early adventure game elements with the wider realm of electronic literature demonstrates the potential of interactive narrative as a primary form rather than as a set of binaries in conflict with one another. The much-debated conflict between interactivity and narrative, like that between ludology and narratalogy, also occurs in discussions of the adventure game, as I've shown, and while as Moulthrop notes it is out of style, the formal tensions remain. It can appear that although these games offer narratives, they are always secondary to the demands of interactivity, since the user is confronted not with a written linear text but with a screen, an interface, a host of characters, and a perspective that differs from game to game. The most important thing about an adventure game is that it must be playable. Playing a game implies an interaction that reading a text does not. A closely related type of criticism is that the stories in computer games are not "literary." In part such comments stem from the assumption that the only good story is a singular, unchanging one to be read. However, computer game stories must be designed to work as part of a whole, subject to interactions of the user. The balance varies across the genre: greater openness comes at the expense of the planned story, while a planned story requires limiting the user's freedom. But what if the user's freedom is not ultimately the goal? What happens when games and fans instead build upon the model suggested by Andrew Plotkin's interactive fiction *Shade*, which deploys interactivity as a tool for the construction of narrative and meaning rather than as an end in itself?

Janet Murray notes that the adventure game worked from its roots to create a feeling of agency: "The adventure maze embodies a classic fairy-tale narrative of danger and salvation. Its lasting appeal as both a story and a game pattern derives from the melding of a cognitive problem (finding the path) with an emotionally symbolic pattern (facing what is frightening and unknown)" (130). During the golden era, the adventure game was still limited by the fairy-tale expectations brought to the game format—the stories resolve happily, the quest through the maze ends with an escape. While the player enjoys a feeling of agency, that feeling is hindered by the foreknowledge of the happily-ever-after ending. These patterns were dominant in the classic model of adventure games but also played a role in setting the stage for the next generation of stories. As players stepped into the shoes of adventure game characters, and became coproducers both of the game experience and of the games as part of transmedia, many brought the same cocreative spirit as Terry Phillips used when breathing life into Raistlin Majere—and these first steps would shape the longer journey of the genre to follow.

CHAPTER 3

King's Quests

THE *KING'S QUEST* SERIES was the most long-running and success-ful series of adventure games published. The lead designer of the *Kings Quest* games was Roberta Williams, whose work post–*Mystery House* extended the integration of graphics meaningfully into the conceptual framework of interactive fiction. The series begins with *King's Quest I: Quest for the Crown*, which has been released in several different ver-sions: the simplified PCjr release in 1983, the PC/Apple II release in 1984, a graphically enhanced version in 1987, a remake in 1990 with improved interface, and an unlicensed remake by fans in 2003. Over the course of this succession, the quality of graphics, sound, and inter-face varies, but the story and puzzles remain the same. The *King's Quest* series is essential to the story of fan production, as it has spawned not only remakes and fan sequels but also one of the most ambitious fan games of all time—released with the copyright holder's permission. The story of *King's Quest*'s evolution paralleled the transformation of inter-active narrative by participatory culture while demonstrating how even a series that began as emblematic of Murray's fairy-tale maze became something greater.

Quest for the Crown offers only a few glimpses of this future signif-icance, as the adventures of Sir Graham began with relatively simple environments and a small playable world. Some of the explanation for the story of *King's Quest I* is not even part of the game itself, but is instead relegated to the manual. In an introductory sequence within the game itself, the king tells Graham of the troubles of the kingdom since the loss of three treasures: a magic mirror, a magic shield, and a chest of infinite gold. If Graham recovers these three treasures, he will inherit the crown and leadership of the kingdom of Daventry, and as the player explores the kingdom it will become clear what a step up this is for Sir Graham, who does not appear to have a house or any belongings of his own upon starting the adventure—he may be a knight, but he doesn't even have a sword (Williams, *King's Quest I*).

As the player leads Sir Graham on his adventures, he moves around on each location screen, but the perspective does not change until he walks on to the next area. The screen that offers the player a view into the world is static, and when he or she moves Graham, it is like moving a puppet on a stage. In the earliest version of *King's Quest I*, the player moved the avatar through text-based commands, such as "look at object" or "walk to object." The later versions change the interface to incorporate the mouse, which offers more graphically based control by allowing the player to click on an object of interest. The player earns points for successful actions that advance the story or solve puzzles. Text command or mouse click, traveling through this land is not without its perils. Opportunities for death exist from the moment Sir Graham steps out of the castle: walk forward too far, and he falls into the moat. A few moments later, a moat monster sticks up a grinning green head—wearing Sir Graham's blue hat. A command box pops up, explaining, "The moat monsters appreciate your good taste." But no death is final, and three options accompany the message: restore, restart, and quit. This is but one of the many ways death can strike Sir Graham. Others include drowning, falling off a cliff, eating a poisonous mushroom, and falling out of the clouds or off a beanstalk.

The game is populated with traditional fantasy creatures: a witch who whisks Graham off and turns him into a gingerbread man ("graham cracker"); an elf with a ring of invisibility; a leprechaun king; a giant who lives in the clouds; and even a fire-breathing dragon. However, as is typical of the adventure games, battle against these enemies is never the focus, although it is possible to engage in violent actions. For instance, the wicked witch can be defeated by pushing her into a boiling pot, and the giant can be defeated through a David and Goliath attack with a slingshot. But these magical villains do not exist merely to be killed; instead, they are puzzles to be solved. These characters reinforce Janet Murray's concept of the early adventure game as maze, owing a debt to the patterns of fairy tales. Many of these archetypes would continue through the early games of the *King's Quest* series—there were eight in total.

PLAYING *KING'S QUEST I*

Solving a puzzle in *King's Quest I* involves moving between several screens and completing specific tasks. For instance, one of the quest items is guarded by a fire-breathing dragon. In order to douse the dragon's flames, a bucket of water would come in handy. There's a bucket hanging from the well—but to get that, you'd have to cut it free from the rope. Unfortunately, Sir Graham is a knight without a sword—a continuity concern that is never explained—so the player has to help him find a dagger. Where do most folks store weaponry? Well, there's a dagger under a rock on another screen, of course. But even that poses a challenge: if Sir Graham tries to push the rock out of the way while standing downhill of it, the player finds himself or herself confronted with another taunting death message: "The moving rock rolls downhill . . . and right into you. A crushing defeat" (Williams, *King's Quest I*). Survive the rock, and you are still only part way to victory over the dragon—with two other treasures waiting to be uncovered throughout the realm.

This interaction of a player with an adventure game world is a good example of what James Paul Gee labels the "probe, hypothesize, reprobe, rethink cycle"—the player clicks on elements in the environment, theorizes about what the objects might mean, attempts to use or interact with the objects based on that hypothesis, and finally gets feedback from the game (90)—hopefully not always with a death message. This same style of gameplay is echoed in *Diamond Age*, to return to Nell's adventures in the Primer:

> "Nell looked for a safe way down," Nell essayed.
> Her vantage point began to move. A patch of snow swung into view.
> "No, wait!" she said, "Nell stuffed some clean snow in her water bottles."
> In the painting, Nell could see her bare pink hands scooping up snow and packing it bit by bit into the neck of her bottle. When it was full, she put the cork back in (Nell didn't have to specify that) and began moving around on the rock, looking for a place that wasn't so steep. Nell didn't have to explain that in detail either; in the ractive, she searched the rock in a fairly rational way and in a few minutes found a stairway chiseled into

the rock, winding down the mountain endlessly until it pierced a cloud
layer far below. (Stephenson 278–279)

Nell's manipulation of the world and its objects through language mir-
rors the interaction of player and text parser in the early adventure
games.

An eventual victory in *King's Quest I* can be won by overcoming all
the obstacles and presenting the three treasures to the king. When this
victory is won, the player—or rather, Sir Graham—will be officially heir
to the throne. However, the final score might not be at a full 158 points.
Even at this early stage of adventure gaming, there were multiple ways
around certain obstacles, and some of those paths are worth more than
others. For instance, the Jack and the Beanstalk–style giant who waits
in a castle in the sky can be killed with a slingshot, but it is worth five
more points to wait for the giant to go to sleep instead (Williams, *King's
Quest I*). The system accommodates different playing styles or moral
codes—that is, it allows for player agency to some degree—but rewards
one style over another, with points as a marker for the quality of a solution. The game also sets up a pattern of failure and repetition that Jane
McGonigal praises in *Reality Is Broken*: "Compared with games, reality is too easy. Games challenge us with voluntary obstacles and help
us put our personal strengths to better use." But however the game is
played, the only conclusion Sir Graham can aim for is ascending to the
throne, again underscoring the underlying limits of the *King's Quest*
narrative.

The pathways through the *King's Quest* games are so fundamentally
linear that they have been easily translated to novellas. Peter Spear's *The
King's Quest Companion* takes the same moments I've just sketched and
provides walkthroughs written as stories with a great deal of narrative
embellishment:

Graham took inventory of what he had. He discovered nothing. That
meant he had to get some food, some gold or the like with which to buy
things, and a weapon. He leaned forward harder and harder, as he set his
plans and sorted out his situation. The rock rolled. Graham stumbled but
a little and, as he recovered his balance, noticed that the rolling stone had

revealed a hole. "Well, it's time to heed some of Daddy's advice," he said to the trees, and looking into the hole, he saw what appeared to be a dagger. So it was, and while taking it he breathed, "Thank you, Father," a note of respect in his voice. "I sure hope this is an omen." (10)

Graham's father (who does not appear in the game) advised Graham to "leave no rock unturned." The player who encounters the game without this guiding narrative is left to wonder at coincidences, such as the dagger conveniently hidden under a rock; the novella adaptation provides a glimpse of some of the underlying logic, and in doing so reveals not only the solutions but more of the context than gameplay alone could hold at this stage of the adventure game's evolution.

One defining aspect of the *King's Quest* series is the development of a storyline in which the central characters, all members of the royal family, age and the playable world expands. The series matures with its protagonist. The first story is, as I've just described, the simple uncomplicated quest of a young man sent to complete three tasks and thus win the throne of the kingdom, an archetypical story repeated throughout mythology. There is no human complication to this first tale, no human rival for the throne. The opponents are all fantastical creatures: a dragon possesses the magic mirror, a giant holds the magical chest, and a leprechaun king has the magic shield. There is not even any implication of moral ambiguity in "repossessing" these items, as the king has declared them to be goods stolen from him. The depth of story in this first game is limited, and so, too, are Sir Graham's wanderings. The entire world seems to consist of screens on an 8 by 6 grid: walk off any edge of the grid, and end up on the other side. Keep walking, and the avatar will always return to where he started. But the later games reflected growing technological and storytelling sophistication.

Perhaps most important, Sir Graham becomes a more complex figure as the games proliferated. The first game of the series begins as the player is introduced to this fairly uncomplicated character: "You are Sir Graham, the bravest and most honorable knight in the troubled realm of Daventry" (Williams, *King's Quest I*). This introduction serves as all the needed backstory for Sir Graham's life prior to his adventure. The avatar of Sir Graham is now iconic—with a pointy blue hat, black hair, red tunic, and knee-high black boots—and initially lacked any specific characteristics or capability of displaying expression. Sir Graham was mostly an iconic male figure left somewhat blank for the projection of the player's own humanity. However, he develops more as a specific character over the course of the series, with each game centering on him and his family as he becomes first the ruler of Daventry and then a husband, father, and aging king. Stepping into Graham's black boots and experiencing Graham as a character at first requires filling in the blanks with the traditions of the questing knightly hero. Graham is singled out by the king as a knight of honor, and the player's first impression of him is through the king's eyes, as the king explains the reasoning behind his choice of Sir Graham as future leader of the realm. Later, when Graham goes on his quest to rescue his future wife, Valanice, he is revealed through her circumstances as a valiant love interest. Through interacting with these characters, the player gets a heroic image of the character he or she inhabits. In later games, players also gained the opportunity to play other characters besides Graham, beginning with *King's Quest III*, where players take the role of Graham's son, Gwydion.

The *King's Quest* series was accompanied by three novels that filled in gaps in the storylines. The first of these novels was released in July 1995. Written by Craig Mills, *The Floating Castle* takes place between games four and six of the adventure game series and features the prince's battle against an evil mage. Both of the remaining novels were written by Kenyon Morr, which is actually a pseudonym for the collaborative team of Mark Sumner and Marcella Sands (Morr, *King's Quest 2*). The second of these novels, *Kingdom of Sorrow*, was published in early 1996 but is set much earlier in the series, between games two and three. The third of these novels, *See No Weevil* (1996), is set seven years after *Kingdom of Sorrow* and relies on the prior story.

The existence of supporting texts, whether those texts are the *King's Quest* novels, *The King's Quest Companion* (1989, print), or the more traditional game manual and supporting explanatory materials, leads to the question of whether an interactive-only adventure game would be possible or if these other styles of storytelling add something essential to the experience that gameplay alone cannot offer. The decision to flesh out the characters of *King's Quest* in novels may have been primarily a marketing decision, an attempt to spin off a successful series, but notably it has been adopted by many similar franchises through today, including *Everquest* (1999, PC) and *World of Warcraft* (2005, PC) among others.

The *King's Quest* novels and games exemplify the distinct strengths of each form of storytelling. Each of these novels offers a story that fleshes out the characters of the series in a way inherently separate from the games themselves. When playing the games, the player has the experience of inhabiting each of the characters of the royal family of Daventry in succession through different installments, while in the novels the player sits outside these characters and watches their journeys as observer rather than participant. But each story of Daventry, whether novel or game, relies on the telling of an epic quest. When this quest is offered in the form of a novel, the reader can interact with the world in a physical sense only by turning the pages. In contrast, the player of an adventure game seems to have a level of control in engaging with the kingdom of Daventry: during most of the game, the main character cannot progress without the action of the player in "moving" the character through the quest.

Despite this level of control, there are moments in the adventure game when the character is no longer under the player's control. These moments are called cut scenes, and they bring an abrupt end to interactivity. The cut scene is often positioned as a reward for moving the storyline forward: when a player overcomes an important obstacle, a cut scene often follows to show how these actions have affected the game. At these points, the experience of the adventure game quest seems to have more in common with a novel or film than with the interactive scenes that make up the rest of the game. No storytelling gaming yet seems to be without these scenes, suggesting that fully interactive gameplay simply does not allow for the same conventions of storytelling, including emotional impact. How are storytelling and engagement with a character's quest different when watching or reading about a character rather than being that character? Cut scenes generally frame the gaming experience at both beginning and end, as well as interrupting play throughout, pushing the player out of the story to watch what his or her choices in the game have brought to pass. From the very start of *King's*

Quest I, the player experiences this passivity as Sir Graham is told by the king of his quest to recover the three magical treasures. Sir Graham listens and accepts the challenge without any input on the part of the player: the player's cooperation and acceptance are assumed. The player cannot interrupt the cinematic arc. In these moments, the character is not an avatar: Sir Graham acts without the player, taking on the role that belongs to him alone within the world.

BEING PRINCESS ROSELLA

The experience of playing an adventure game is not the direct experience of being the central character in the game. The player is interacting with the game, but it is not the player's image that is on the screen. As I noted earlier, this separation of avatar and player stems from the clear physical difference in the body: "the long history of video games also makes clear that there is no perfectly 'reflective' avatar, that is, one that resembles the player visually and . . . seems to gaze back on him or her" (Rehak 107). Nevertheless, throughout all the events of an adventure game, the player inhabits a particular and generally consistent body. The playable character is a specific avatar, not a generic stand-in for the player. Most important, the avatar is not an empty shell.

This personality on the part of the playable character is most often reflected in actions by the avatar on objects or people in the environment. The avatar reveals the world through a "look" function, which varies slightly from game to game but is always present. The same function existed before animated adventure games in text-only games, where in response to the typed command "look at object," the player gets to read the avatar's opinion on the object in question. In text-only games, this is the only description available. The "look" function in an animated adventure game is more complex, as objects and characters are identified with descriptive text but are also available in visual representations as graphics on the screen. This descriptive text reflects the views and experience of the avatar being inhabited; in a game in which multiple characters are playable, the text produced when the player has the avatar look at an object will change to reflect each character. For example, in *Maniac Mansion* each character's reaction to picking up an in-game manuscript of the main villain's biography is different; the writer Wendy makes the most evaluative analysis, drawing on her training, commenting, "It looks like someone's memoir . . . but the writing is terrible." A description without the perspective of the character would be bland: for instance, the manuscript might be described as "a handwritten document." That sort of text would reflect only the first half of a process of observation, the aspect of taking in details visually, but it would not reflect the specific experience of this particular eye and mind processing information—it would remain a cold and distant description, omniscient rather than particular to the perspective occupied by the player within the world.

We can see the difference a different avatar makes by examining some of the *King's Quest* games in which the avatar is someone other than Sir Graham. In *King's Quest IV*, the avatar is Princess Rosella. At the beginning of the game, Rosella's father, King Graham, has decided he is too old for adventuring. He is ready to hand off that iconic blue hat from his own questing days to his children. He has two, a son and a daughter, but he does not distinguish between the two in his desire to see them go adventuring. His son Gwydion's adventure preceded this installment, so his perspective is already familiar to the player of the series at this point. But at the moment when Graham is passing the hat to his children, his own weakness and age are revealed as he suffers from a crippling heart failure—and it is his daughter, Rosella, who goes off in search of a cure (Williams, *King's Quest IV*).

Princess Rosella is also the central character in the third *King's Quest* novel, *See No Weevil*. The novel begins with Rosella's decision to have a stump moved out of the way of a harvest festival she is planning, despite warnings from the castle seneschal: "Don't you know there's an old legend saying disaster will come to Daventry if the stump is removed?" (Morr, *King's Quest 3* 29). The reader may be unsurprised by the chaos that follows. The remaining story is the tale of Rosella's attempt to deal with two threats to the kingdom, a pack of vicious lizards and invading magical bugs called weevils that escape from beneath the stump. Throughout the text she continually reminds the reader of her status as a particular character, even when she engages in the mundane task of choosing her daily wardrobe: "The blue dress Rosella was to have worn to the wedding banquet caught her eye. She ran her hand down the skirt of the dress. . . . The pearls helped some, but the dress still looked lacy and frilly in all the wrong ways. It looked like a little girl's dress. Nothing in her wardrobe seemed really appropriate for a person in control of a kingdom" (9). Her choices mark her as a woman of wealth and status, a princess in a magical land, and a young woman trying to enter the adult world. The reader may or may not identify with any of these qualities, but even to the extent that they are qualities the reader possesses, they are still here intensely connected to another person. The reader does not choose what Rosella wears, and the reader, if pressed to do so, may not endorse the decisions that Rosella makes. She is a complete character entirely separate from the reader, who may well be reading the stories of the adventuring princess wearing nothing more formal than blue jeans.

For the purposes of enjoying a fantasy, this is as expected. A story of this nature offers the reader the opportunity to act as a voyeur, watching a life that is different from the reader's own and thus hopefully intriguing. The reader continues to share the experience of Rosella's wardrobe choices throughout the novel:

> Rosella flipped through the dresses, looking for something that didn't look so much like a little girl's dress. And then she saw it. Way in the back of the wardrobe. An emerald-green overdress with gold-thread piping and delicate lace at the waist, neck, and cuffs. A cream-colored underdress hung next to it. Next to that was a silken cream-colored belt. Rosella gasped. This was one of her mother's dresses. She couldn't remember Valanice wearing it recently, but it definitely was a dress for a queen, not a young princess. (Morr, *King's Quest 3* 65)

These novels emphasize Rosella's coming of age, paralleling the youth-driven focus of the *CYOA* books.

In *King's Quest IV*, the adventure game setting offers Princess Rosella as the playable character. The player, like the reader, has no say in Rosella's wardrobe. The player's own feelings on the appropriateness of pearls or dresses for going on a quest are never sought. Instead, the player takes the avatar "as is," without any ability to tailor the character on the screen to suit his or her liking. This take-it-or-leave-it avatar is not typical of other styles of games, which may offer many characters to choose from and whose stories might be less dependent on the avatar's developed personal identity. But in an adventure narrative, the quest depends on the avatar—in this case, on Rosella being who she is, pearls and all. Throughout the game the players see the defined avatar of Rosella with her blonde hair and red dress. This is the primary image of Rosella that the player encounters throughout the game, and while it is a low-resolution cartoon depiction, it does envision Rosella as the other, both in a body and in a location separate from the player. In contrast, when reading the book the reader may imagine Rosella differently, as the character is embodied in words rather than in a moving image.

In contrast, in the game Rosella responds to the player's hand in a way that a page in a book cannot. Whether the player is using typed commands, such as "pick up" or "push," or arrow keys, or a mouse to control movement, the player is in effect a puppeteer: his or her hand may not directly equate to Rosella's hand, but a gesture from the player sets Rosella's hand in motion. Thus when the character finds herself trapped within the belly of a whale in her trials in *King's Quest IV*, it is the player who sends her hand reaching out with a feather to tickle the whale and allows her escape (Williams, *King's Quest IV*). The princess will wait trapped indefinitely within this space without the player's guidance. Her story is programmed with multiple possibilities, and which outcome is reached depends dynamically on the input of the player. Rosella here is almost inactive: the character has no agency in her own fate. A character with agency would be allowed motivation of her own to escape and change circumstances, but Rosella is not given that privilege: the player's agency is her loss.

When Rosella finds herself trapped within the novel *See No Weevil*, her initial circumstances are similar. She is lost within the Old Woods, and the fairies lure her into the woods to lie down on the moss and sleep away her life. Rosella is drawn in by the voices, and by page 164 of the novel she is in great danger: "A soft listlessness drifted over Rosella. She felt very tired, more exhausted than she had been even after the horrible day of burning weevils. Perhaps a long, long nap here on the soft mossy ground would be the best thing. It really was a pretty spot" (Morr,

King's Quest 3 164). If the reader stops reading at that exact moment, the story itself doesn't change. The novel is complete already. The reader chooses only whether to advance his or her own experience of the novel. This can mean choosing to turn to page 165 or continuing on to read the next chapter, but it does not mean choosing an action. In a sense, this Rosella has more agency than the Rosella of the game: the novel tells readers about her thought processes, her attempts to save herself by fighting against various obstacles, and the outcomes of those fights. Thus Rosella's actions are being held up for the reader to consider and engage with, not to change. The author is ultimately in control of the character's agency within a book, but that control is relaxed and shared in the game.

Reading on for a few paragraphs reveals the rest of Rosella's fate: the fairy queen emerges to free her. On one level, it does not matter for the reader whether Rosella saves herself or whether the fairy queen acts to save her—either action is equally separate from the action of the reader, who is simply continuing to follow a story that is already set on paper. On another level, however, the reader has to consider the implications of Rosella needing to be saved from this particular obstacle—the fairy queen here has as much control over Rosella as the player does over Rosella the avatar. When the avatar is confronted with an equally menacing forest in *King's Quest IV*, the player has to find a way to defeat the threatening trees, while the princess seems dwarfed and overwhelmed by them. The player has an entire area to search to find a solution to the imposing threat and must logically determine that an ax might be the appropriate tool for the situation, and then acquire the ax. That turns out to be a complicated task, as it requires the player to lead Rosella in outrunning and distracting a bulldog and then grabbing the necessary tool. At each moment of this task, failure is possible if the player misleads Rosella or chooses to abandon the task.

The ability of the player to overcome the trees could be put down to a matter of scale, understood almost as divine interference. To Rosella, the trees are menacing and overwhelming, overpowering in their size. But to the player, these trees are merely small cartoon depictions on the monitor sitting in front of him or her, and thus conquerable. The player therefore acts as the hand of fate in Rosella's life, and can through success or failure doom the princess to destruction by those trees. A vindictive player might choose to watch Rosella die over and over again, using the "save game" command that allows perpetual resurrection as a way to enjoy watching the avatar suffer. In order to be motivated to continue to guide Rosella until she saves her father and finishes her quest safely, the player has to be invested in the avatar's fate, just as the reader has to be invested in a character to be motivated to finish a novel. There are many ways games try to create that investment, one of which is through the simple challenge of completion—a player should want to help Rosella acquire the ax and conquer the forest because there is a pleasure in that victory and a reward in score and advancement. But this is a reflexive connection, not necessarily an investment, and the adventure game's prolonged exercise in narrative should make a deeper one possible. *King's Quest IV* aspires to that deeper connection by trying to engage the player with Rosella's fate through emotional investment—again, like a novel does—rather than simply the desire for success.

CUT SCENES AND AGENCY

As I noted earlier, cut scenes in computer games bear a surface resemblance to animated films. Examining the convergence of games and films critically faces the same limitations as studying the convergence of games and novels, as Bernard Perron observed when bringing the lens of film studies to games such as the interactive movie/adventure horror game *Phantasmagoria* (Sierra 1995). *Phantasmagoria* offered an avatar played by an actress, Victoria Morsell, but it could not be filmed in any traditional way. Designer Roberta Williams described some of the challenges her team of developers faced, such as keeping Morsell's character, Adrienne, in the same outfit for multiple days: "The reason she wears the same clothes for several days is because this is an adventure game rather than a movie. In a movie, the scriptwriter can control the action, the days, wardrobe, etc. In an adventure game, the player is much more in control than the scriptwriter. Therefore, the player can have Adrienne do whatever he or she wants (to a great extent) throughout the game" (Bellatti). Roberta Williams was keenly aware of the challenge of interactivity versus narrative: "I could put a tighter rein on gameplay (read, interactivity) and not allow much decision on the part of the player to have Adrienne 'do' things, thereby allowing many more costume changes on the part of Adrienne; or I could allow more decision-making on the part of the player in regards to Adrienne, but not allow any costume changes" (Bellatti). The resulting game includes hours of film that the player might never see, as Victoria Morsell was filmed against a blue screen performing every action Williams included. The resulting horror game is a playable video with the player as codirector, cycling through the prefilmed repertoire of actions.

Just as when literary critics compared novels with games, when film critics compare games to movies the games do not fare well, quite aside from criticisms of poor acting and storytelling in the games. Perron argued that games suffer from what he calls a "closed interactivity" in which all outcomes are determined and the player merely flips between scripted moments. Perron furthermore claimed: "it is not possible to tell a story by putting the storytelling in the hands of the spectator," suggesting that to even use the lens of film studies (or, by extension, narrative studies) to look at games is self-defeating—"it is certainly not the film or the narrative part that is worth examining" (239). Despite Perron's criticism, the game was one of the best-selling PC games of its year, and many other adventure games have also borrowed formal structures from film and repurposed them for interactive storytelling. Clearly they are doing something that players like, even if it does not qualify as good literature or good cinema.

In graphical adventure games, such scenes are typically accomplished through animation, in part because it would be difficult for an actor to perform the huge possible range of actions necessary in order to provide for all the user's possible choices. But cut scenes limit activity and put the player in the role of a viewer, making the film comparison inevitable. And indeed, game designers use cut scenes precisely to develop the kind of emotional complexity associated with feature-length films. There is no better example of this than Sierra's advertising for *King's Quest IV*, which established the emotional stakes of the game in the opening cut scene, in which the quest is first established when Rosella's father suffers a heart attack:

> When *King's Quest IV* debuted in front of a live audience, the face of com-
> puter entertainment was changed forever. The scene began with a soul-
> stirring orchestration, lifted to a triumphant chorus, and then elevated
> to the heralded announcement of trumpets as the hero, King Graham,
> entered the scene. The eyes of everyone in the room were mesmerized to
> the screen as the lifelike King appeared on screen, breathtakingly detailed
> from the tranquil look in his eyes to the growing creases upon his fore-
> head. Suddenly, the revered silence was filled by gasps of shock around
> the room as King Graham suddenly slumped to the floor. Moments later,
> when the lights came up, one could see the mist that yet lingered in the
> spectators' eyes. Even more startling, tears were found screaming down
> the face of a woman in the third row. (Sierra On-Line)

Sierra trumpeted this powerful cut scene as a step in a new direction toward more complex storytelling than previous adventure games had offered. The purpose of this scene was to give the game an emotional urgency that would inspire the player to feel invested in pushing Rosella's quest forward.

Contrast this scene with the opening of the first *King's Quest* game, in which a matter-of-fact aging king sends Sir Graham off to recover three stolen artifacts with no particular urgency but the lure of the throne. The story never develops beyond that initial sequence, as every interaction from that point on occurs simply through recovering the objects. By contrast, the quest to save King Graham in *King's Quest IV* is loaded with emotional drama, from the opening scene to the placing of a character that the player might have controlled in previous *King's Quest* games in jeopardy. The player's powerlessness in the cinematic opening scene echoes Rosella's own: the player and Rosella can only watch King Graham's initial descent into illness. However, both gain agency by going on a quest to save him. Several traditional themes are present to tie the beginning of this story to stories with emotional resonance, chief among them the quest of a daughter to save her father.

The ability of players to lose themselves in Rosella's desires can best be termed "immersion." Janet Murray defines this term by referring to the concrete sensation it initially named: "Immersion is a metaphorical term derived from the physical experience of being submerged in water.

. . . In a participatory medium, immersion implies learning to swim, to do the things that the new environment makes possible" (98). In an adventure game, immersion means taking on the dual roles of learning the logic of the story, and thus of the puzzles, and accepting and participating in the character's quest. Often, games are judged on their ability to provide both elements of immersion. Although critics accuse moments such as cut scenes of interrupting that immersion, such cinematic moments remain powerful and necessary because they deliver narrative information and character emotion outside of direct player control.

Moments of emotional resonance read very differently in the accompanying *King's Quest* novels. Rosella's quest in the novel is imperiled by sloks, fierce and hungry lizard creatures who provide similar moments of potential tragedy for the reader to become invested in. During one of these moments, the reader discovers that one of Rosella's friends is wounded at the same time that she does:

> William turned his head, and Rosella was startled to see an expression of pain on his face. "Did the others make it back?" "Others?" Rosella shook her head in confusion. "What others?" "The others that were working with me," he said. "I sent them back when we were attacked." William climbed to his feet and Rosella saw that a torn piece of cloth was wrapped around one arm. . . . The cloth, which Rosella now saw was a torn shirt, was dotted with blood. She pushed his hands away and peeled the shirt from his arm. Beneath was a red semicircle of wounds. (Morr, *King's Quest 3* 121)

The emotional difference of the two sequences lies in part in perspective. When watching the cut scene of the game, the player first sees a close-up of King Graham's face viewed from the same angle as Rosella, standing across from him. The camera then shifts to show the full scene from the side, with Rosella and her brother rushing forward as Graham collapses. This distance from Rosella allows the player to witness her pain and therefore to understand her motivation throughout the quest, a motivation that the story relies upon the player accepting somewhat as his or her own. The player sees the events through his or her own eyes, not entirely through Rosella's. While the novel is not narrated in first person and thus also does not place the player immediately in Rosella's thoughts and perspective, its limited third-person narration follows Rosella closely and offers information only as Rosella processes it, colored with her own perspective—the reader does not get told anything that Rosella does not know. The reader cannot sit back objectively when William is first found and determine from the cloth around his arm that he is injured; instead, the player is dependent upon Rosella's analysis of the situation. This is a very traditional experience of narrative: in his essay "Stories for the Eye, Ear, and Muscles: Video Games, Media, and Embodied Experiences," Torben Grodal defines a story as "a sequence of events focused by one . . . living being," in this case Rosella, and thus "the events are based on simulations of experiences in which there is a constant interaction of perceptions, emotions, cognitions and actions" (130). This interaction of perceptions and experiences is complicated by the juxtaposition of Rosella's experience and knowledge with those of the reader and the reader's ability to make conclusions both contrary to those Rosella might reach and about Rosella herself.

Grodal notes that this traditional model of storytelling has to change when the story platform is moved to the computer: "The computer story . . . is only developed by the player's active participation, and the player needs to possess a series of specific skills to 'develop' the story, from concrete motor skills and routines to a series of planning skills" (139). In a sense, Rosella in book form operates from her own mind, making decisions and determinations, such as about William's state of health. In the gameplay, however, the player is Rosella's mind: the player has to analyze a situation and determine what steps need to be taken to reach the goal of saving her father. The player is assumed to share Rosella's desire, or at least to accept Rosella's desire, because that decision is the only one that advances the gameplay—if the player were to decide *not* to go on the quest to find Graham's cure, there would be no game to play, no story to experience, no emotional conflict to experience.

Ironically, this motivation has to be inspired by a cut scene that sets the stakes of the game. The opening cut scene in *King's Quest IV* dramatizes this irony by mirroring it. The scene presents a fairy, who appears in a mirror and whose blonde hair and white dress reflect Rosella's own image back to her, to give Rosella the opportunity to take an active role in her father's health. The juxtaposition of the fairy on a blue screen, the mirror, with Rosella looking at her to learn what the quest will be echoes the positioning of the player sitting before another screen looking in. This moment of reflection sets in motion the remaining sequences: Rosella takes the quest to find her father's cure, and the player joins her.

Like many game critics, Grodal notes that moments such as this when the video game approaches the style of film "temporarily block interaction . . . such sequences in a video game are experienced in a context of interaction, they are experienced as more 'dead,' less 'vivid' than in a film context" (144). Chris Crawford agrees that in cut scenes the entire dynamic of gaming is lost, but he also acknowledges that such moments may have great emotional power:

> In Infocom's classic game *Planetfall*, Floyd the robot befriended players early in the game. Floyd helped out in all manner of ways and provided lots of humorous diversions. But then, in a moment of danger to the player, Floyd charged forward and sacrificed himself to save the player. Players were overwhelmed with the moment's emotional power. This great moment, I must point out, does not meet any definition for interactivity. There was nothing players could do to avert it. Players could insult Floyd, abuse Floyd, ignore Floyd, and he'd still nobly sacrifice himself. (337)

Indeed, most of the classic story moments of adventure games, such as the death of Floyd in *Planetfall* (1983, DOS/Apple II), occur in the same fashion as an event in a movie: players can only observe them, not change them. However, does the cut scene have to be so easily dismissed as resorting to cinematic tricks to evoke the emotional resonance that the game supposedly cannot offer? It is true that this moment is not interactive, but perhaps its power is in the lack of interactivity. If the player could save Floyd in the same way that the player can reload the game each time Rosella dies, then Floyd's death would be meaningless, simply another challenge to be overcome and moved past. But by making Floyd's death inevitable, the game evokes human empathy and the reality that sometimes there is nothing to be done.

Powerlessness is part of storytelling. In *Stranger than Fiction* (2006, film), Will Ferrell plays a character in someone else's novel who has realized he is facing his own death. His progress through the story is narrated until he gains enough self-awareness to confront his puppet master, eventually forestalling death not through his own actions but through the author's decision to rewrite the plot. Recall Andrew Plotkin's interactive fiction work *Shade*, in which the player can search for a way out of the desert mirage. But the player cannot signal a helicopter, cannot change the decision that brought him or her into the desert in the first place; the player is always moving toward the same final ending. The ending of *Shade* could be called a playable cut scene: the outcome is fixed, and the player's emotional journey lies in coming to terms with his or her powerlessness. The player can walk away or choose new ways to struggle, but only Andrew Plotkin can rewrite the ending itself. But if this deterministic quality of gameplay renders the player powerless, then interactivity is an illusion. Yet the player's choices *can* change the game world. In Emily Short's interactive fiction *Bronze*, a retelling of "Beauty and the Beast," the player's choices can lead to multiple endings with different outcomes for the Beast, the villagers, and the other residents of the Beast's castle. While *Shade* experiments with the futility of play in the face of death, *Bronze* rejects the finality of its narrative inspiration.

There is another emotion the cut scene can convey, one that is easily conveyed in the text of the novel. This is the emotion of desire, and it can be as simple as the princess daydreaming of something that would make her life more satisfying: "Rosella's ears perked up at [the mention of magic]. Her father had never allowed her to be involved with any sort of magic. Maybe, with Farquhar's aid, she could try her hand at it. Maybe one day she could be a powerful sorceress queen, able to conjure with a gesture or curse with a sneeze" (Morr, *King's Quest 3* 20). These desires can also be more complex, romantic desires, which the reader may or may not share with Rosella but can empathize with when they are revealed: "William was several years older than Rosella and several inches taller. His cocky good looks sent the maids swooning after him. Rosella pretended not to notice, but she occasionally caught herself watching him, too. That annoyed her. William was only a seneschal's son, never destined to rise to greater heights than the office his father now occupied. Rosella was a princess and entirely beyond his station"

(Morr, *King's Quest 3* 14). This may not be pure interactivity, but it engages the player with the character's situation and struggle, using the "play" with emotions and engagement that is associated with text just as puzzles and obstacles are associated with games.

HAPPY ENDINGS

As an avatar, Rosella may possess desires that the player might not share, and the cinematic cut scene can be a means for inciting the reader to experience these desires. Players who aid in Rosella's quest are granted a final emotional payoff: Rosella and the rest of the family gather around a revitalized King Graham, beaming with happiness, in the final cut scene of the game. Here the rules of the game system correspond with the demands of the narrative: "a player makes a goal-oriented choice and the game provides a meaningful outcome" (Salen and Zimmerman). As shown in plate 3, the player's victory is reflected by the smiling face of the avatar.

These last moments of the game offer an emotional counterpart to the opening sequence, an uplifting conclusion to follow the grim beginning. However, the sequence is not without its emotional complexity. In one of the final cut scenes of *King's Quest IV* (1988, DOS/Apple II), Rosella faces the problem of a budding relationship with Edgar, the man who escaped from the evil fairy's castle with her and who now is professing his love to her. But to return Edgar's love and stay with him in the fairy kingdom would mean not returning to stand by her father. As with Floyd's death in *Planetfall*, witnessing the character's internal struggle without being able to quickly make the choice for Rosella might here make for a more powerful sequence than an interactive one, because, as Crawford noted, "there was nothing players could do to avert it" (337). In the end, the princess chooses to reject Edgar's love and return to her family. This layering is part of an early attempt to create a game that is also a story of complexity, in which the happy ending is not without its less happy consequences and the character is not defined only by the one dimension of success in an initial easily defined quest.

The experience of playing Rosella is the experience of taking over for her mind, but it is not yet the experience of taking over for her heart. Inducing a person to experience the desire of someone removed from himself or herself and his or her own situation is a fundamental challenge and power of any form of storytelling, whether a novel or computer game. This is why computer games today continue to use cut scenes despite the critics' complaint that they are noninteractive by nature. Juxtaposing the games with the *King's Quest* novels shows that these cut scenes echo some of the novels' strength in offering moments of character development that provide perspective while evoking empathy, not interaction. They are a powerful tool for communicating emotion and desire and for showing actions by a character that belong to that character, not to the player. As one reviewer notes looking back on *King's Quest IV*: "KQ [*King's Quest*] IV broke new ground, both with its female protagonist and its relationship-driven plot. It may not have withstood the last two decades as the emotional powerhouse that Sierra claimed in their ads, but the game did explore interpersonal relationships with a depth that few, if any, games had up to this point" (Morganti par. 2). This emotional resonance was a pivotal part of the game's advertising campaign.

And Sierra did not cease to innovate with Rosella's quest to save her father. In some of the games, there is the possibility of an alternative "unhappy" ending, as in *King's Quest VII: The Princeless Bride* (1994, DOS/Windows/Mac). While the object of the quest is not marriage, the final destination for Rosella is toward romance with Edgar, a character from *King's Quest IV* who returns in his true form to court his first love. It is Rosella who helps break the curse on him rather than the other way around, and this after refusing him in *King's Quest IV* in favor of returning to help her father. In *King's Quest VII*, Rosella continues her trend of acting as rescuer, and the implication is that Rosella "wins" Edgar as her reward for her virtue throughout. Edgar exists as a prize, one that Rosella refused at the end of *King's Quest IV* in favor of returning to save her father. Now, years later in the arc of the story, Rosella doesn't have to make any sacrifices to have Edgar—except, as the player may notice watching this "happy ending" unfold, she must sacrifice her desire for adventure and independence in favor of eventual bonding within the traditions of royalty and marriage. The player's failure to rescue Edgar results in the game ending without Rosella being reunited with her love interest. But the player's initiative is limited here. If he or she rescues Edgar, the player cannot decide that Rosella might be happy to see him live but not particularly interested in a relationship: the endings represent only the two binary paths. Moreover, the ending cut scene indicates that the ending in which Edgar and Rosella are not reunited is indeed a failure, a less fortuitous path through the game. The player can determine the outcome, but he or she cannot recode the implication that Rosella without her supposed love interest is less happy than Rosella reunited with him. This structure of choices seems all the more curious because at the outset of the game, Rosella indicated her desire to live free of the constraints a husband would place on her life. Is the player's agency in the adventure game as illusory as the woman's apparent agency once she has escaped a physical prison for the socially constructed one of a medieval-style wedding?

Of course, the possibility of the unhappy ending in *King's Quest VII* is minimized in part by the fact that the mistake is easily undone: "In videogames, regret is an easily vanquishable phantom; it operates merely as a fleeting wound that may be quickly salved" (Poole 224). If Rosella fails at first to rescue Edgar during the course of the game, the player can always undo that failure. The ability to reload a game eliminates the element of tragedy from death or failure—"great stories depend for their effect on irreversibility—and this is because life, too, is irreversible" (Poole 99). The same meaninglessness cheapens any death that cuts short gameplay. In the *King's Quest* series, death might lurk around any corner and strike down Rosella or her mother, Valanice, on their way to find a happy ending, but the reload button always erases the loss. Once again we see the narrative value of cut scenes: the emotions they evoke cannot be avoided.

CHAPTER 4

Epitaph for a Genre?

OUTSIDE OF THE KINGDOM of Daventry, the world of videogames was changing. Increased processing power and better-funded game development enabled the introduction of 3-D computer graphics, and the demand for greater spectacle and improved aesthetics shaped the next generation of adventure games at both Sierra and LucasArts, at times attracting criticism that storylines were being neglected. Following the full-motion-video adventure game *Phantasmagoria* (1995, PC/Sega Saturn), which I mentioned earlier, Sierra released *Phantasmagoria: A Puzzle of Flesh* (1996, DOS/Windows)—also known as *Phantasmagoria II: Fatal Obsessions* in some releases. The latter game bore no resemblance in story or character to the original, unlike the evolving narrative of the *King's Quest* series. The game was very poorly received, and one reviewer criticized it for lacking a good story: "*Phantasmagoria: A Puzzle of Flesh* takes giant steps back, both as a game and as an interactive experience. The film quality is far superior to either of its predecessors, but technical achievements don't amount to much when it seems like the story was written for the Halloween issue of a junior high school newspaper" (Dulin). The story relies heavily on cut scenes to explain a convoluted plot involving the playable character, Curtis Craig, defending himself against accusations of murder a year after his release from a mental institution. The cause of the murders is revealed through those cut scenes to be a manifestation of the "real" Curtis Craig, trapped in an alien dimension and using psychic powers. The game definitely defies any expectations of a happy ending: Curtis is given the choice between staying on Earth (in which case he kills his girlfriend, possessed by his other self) or leaving Earth forever. This is the only meaningful decision the player makes, perhaps in part because, unlike the previous *Phantasmagoria*, the game was prefilmed on location without as much room for player controls. In an interview the game's designer, Ken Williams, assigned the game part of the blame for the eventual fall of Sierra as an adventure game titan—and perhaps part of the blame for the death of the genre itself:

> I always thought the future of storytelling was on the computer. I predicted that computer games would be bigger than films, and still believe there is huge potential with story-telling games—if done correctly. Watching a story from the inside is more exciting than from the outside. Phantasmagoria was a first step towards where I thought the future was. It's disappointing that we blew it with Phantasmagoria II and shot the category. (Schneider)

Ken Williams refers to the category of adventure games—the future of storytelling that he had predicted, with the original *Phantasmagoria*'s fusion of film and play as a successful example of what adventure games could learn from other media. The changes in the industry correspond with the discourse surrounding the aesthetics of the time. Steven Poole observed games during the transition to 3-D as driven by motion: "A beautifully designed videogame invokes wonder as the fine arts do, only in a uniquely kinetic way. Because the videogame must move, it cannot offer the lapidary balance of composition that we value in painting; on the other hand, because it can move, it is a way to experience architecture, and more than that to create it, in a way with which photographs or drawings can never compete" (226). This comment recalls Bolter and Grusin's concept of remediation, but it also points to a critique of adventure games as "games." Adventure games did not seem to be keeping pace with this kinetic landscape because they focused on puzzles, not reflexes.

By contrast, Poole considered the videogame as of 2000 stuck in an early stage of development, namely realism: videogames were focused on making the world on the screen more realistic, rather than exploring the potential of the unreal. He saw this insistence on realism as a step backward from the early games in which "the abstract, voidal spaces . . . were in some senses far more interesting than the third-hand patchwork worlds of the majority of current exploration games. But there, modernist abstraction was a happy by-product, born of technological necessity" (Poole 218). Early computer graphics capabilities had been minimal and games had to make do with very simple line drawings or all-text-centered environments, whereas after 2000 or so, players expected a fully fleshed 3-D environment that looks real enough to touch. It might seem that realistic game worlds would enhance the adventure games by adding depth to their storytelling and puzzle possibilities. However, they did not seem to; instead, in the case of failures like *Phantasmagoria: A Puzzle of Flesh*, the realism detracted from the sense of play. The four hours of film were too movielike and set for responsiveness and interactivity.

Poole argues that the next stage of development should be a fundamental rethinking of the rules: "Designers ought to have the courage to play with the very fabric of their unreality, to create ever newer kinds of space rather than settling permanently on scientific perspective—itself, as we have seen, a tissue of illusionistic distortions" (215). Instead of trying to model physics engines and graphics to be as true to real life as possible, he calls for an "unreal" real: "We are everywhere alienated from nature in the real world, but for a time we can feel oddly at home in this unreal universe, where our strengths can always overcome our difficulties" (Poole 212). After all, as Poole points out, many elements of gaming do not conform to the expectation of realism, creating a discontinuity in the game: "A world can't be built in isolation. Every facet of the videogame development process is organically interrelated with the requirements of the others" (212). *Phantasmagoria: A Puzzle of Flesh's* combination of a real-seeming world with aliens, psychic encounters, and a disconnect between interface and possible actions and the stiffness of the prerecorded sequences is an example of that type of discontinuity, where realism could not yet convincingly convey the surreal elements on which the game relied. However, an "unreal" real was already emerging in other facets of the adventure game genre, though it would be some time before it became fully apparent as one aspect of the aesthetic revival that awaited the adventure game genre.

THE END OF *KING'S QUEST*?

With the failure of *Phantasmagoria: A Puzzle of Flesh* in 1996, Sierra struggled with a new market filled with the first generation of 3-D game worlds and tried to inject new life into even its most classic franchise. Rosella's journeys in *King's Quest IV* and *King's Quest VII* would mark the end of Sierra's commitment to the royal family of Daventry's adventures by returning to the kingdom of Daventry but through a new, unrelated avatar. With 3-D graphics, objects have more definite form, as is seen in *King's Quest VIII: Mask of Eternity* (1998, Windows PC), the first game in the series with the new graphics. At the same time that Sierra was transforming the *King's Quest* franchise, greater changes in the industry were occurring that undermined the company. Increasingly, players pushed aside adventure games in favor of action games such as *Doom*, in which combat is the main focus. Sierra and its rival, LucasArts, mostly abandoned the industry, and smaller companies came to dominate the adventure game genre, their new releases targeted toward a smaller audience of established adventure game fans.

Fans of the genre were less than thrilled with the changes to the genre that accompanied some of the corresponding "action adventure" efforts such as *Indiana Jones and the Infernal Machine* (1999, Windows PC/Nintendo 64), efforts that seemed to abandon some of the principles that had previously governed the genre—and were successful in doing so, despite disappointing the adventure game fan base. As one reviewer noted of the game, "Any gamer who is hoping to settle down for a relaxing graphic adventure game with lots of character interactions is going to be sorely disappointed. The truth is that there is not very much character interaction in this game, an area which I feel has been somewhat neglected" (Howe 7). These new games retained the idea of a central predetermined avatar at the center of the story but brought in the elements of action and combat. Sierra switched to this form with the last *King's Quest* game, which fans denounced as no longer true to the *King's Quest* tradition: as Rosemary Young said in her review at the time, "though you do get a glimpse of the old *King's Quest*, you also get a good dose of *Tomb Raider*, or any of the other dozens of hack and slash titles, and in the Gnome's underground world there's a lot of the feeling of a roleplaying game complete with levers and pits and rolling rocks." However, the game also received many positive reviews and accolades (including Adventure Game of the Year nominations), which suggested this was indeed the future of the genre. The message seemed clear: adventure game mechanics were no longer sufficient. There were no further official releases in the *King's Quest* series.

However, players used to adventuring with Sir Graham's family were not so ready to give up on it, and even as other companies joined Sierra in moving away from the adventure game form, player-creators devoted to it would not only make Sir Graham walk again in 2-D worlds reimagined or extended from the series legacy but also, in time, they would bring Sir Graham and his family back to life in 3-D graphics in a work of interactive narrative referred to for some time as *King's Quest IX*. This was the silver lining of a coming storm that would force the adventure game out of the commercial industry that birthed it.

ABANDONED STORIES

Roberta and Ken Williams sold Sierra On-Line in 1996 and left shortly after, before the studio they'd built was mostly shut down in 1999. High expectations for sales had brought several new developers to the genre, and the mass exodus also brought many of their projects to a crashing halt. Several adventure game projects, including the next titles in Al Lowe's *Leisure Suit Larry* (1987–2009, PC and various) and Scott Murphy's *Space Quest* (1986–1995, PC and various) series, were canceled—both games would have involved at least some 3-D, not unlike *King's Quest VIII*. But the market had changed, and the new owners of Sierra saw no market to justify continuing the adventure game genre. It didn't help that *Grim Fandango* (Windows), Tim Schaffer's 1998 LucasArts release—following in the spirit of *Maniac Mansion*, but featuring a 3-D exploration of the Land of the Dead—failed to impress in sales while winning over critics. However, the game is notable for holding hints of an unreal real, with striking visuals illustrating the adventure of Manny, travel agent in the Department of the Dead, as he tries to save a new soul whom he believes deserves a quick path to eternal bliss. In other respects, the game design document for *Grim Fandango* is a testament to its reliance on the structures of the genre, and particularly the adventure game puzzle (Schafer, Tsacle, and Ingerson). The outline shows the potential branches in the narrative based on the order in which the player collects objects, interacts with characters, and tackles puzzles—always reconverging on the linear narrative path.

Despite *Grim Fandango*'s combination of fidelity to the form with 3-D graphics, the final *King's Quest* had better sales numbers. These failures (when contrasted with some of the relative success of *King's Quest IX: Mask of Eternity* and the resilience of the role-playing genre) only gave weight to the belief in the gaming industry that the traditional adventure game was dead and a new hybrid was ultimately more viable commercially. Although Roberta Williams had designed *King's Quest VIII*, its integration of action reflected her own concerns that in the face of the changing market the genre needed something new to stay alive—though ultimately the transformations resulted in a new genre rather than in an extended life for the traditional form. With the commercial abandonment of the adventure game, many of the great designers of the genre's golden age were now out of a job, and the seemingly unstoppable *King's Quest* series came to an end. The ramifications for the genre rippled through the industry. When projects were canceled, only their evocative screenshot remains were left on the Internet as a monument to their designers' intentions.

One such abandoned project, pictured in plate 4, shows the potential evolution of comic styling in the genre crossed with an already popular franchise. In the mid-1990s, Blizzard Entertainment announced that it was going to enter the adventure game genre with an installment of its popular *Warcraft* franchise, which had previously taken the form of two real-time strategy games, *Warcraft* (1994, DOS/Mac) and *Warcraft II: Tides of Darkness* (1996, PC/Mac/Sega Saturn/Playstation). In 1998, it announced that even though the project was essentially complete, the company had decided to cancel it. In an interview with *Gamespot* magazine, designer Bill Roper explained the decision:

> I can't speak for everybody, but a large group of us really love adventure games and have a desire to do an adventure game. And also I think that the adventure game is still the single best way to tell a story. I think that what an adventure game is, is going to start changing, if it hasn't already. I think that one of the big problems with *Warcraft Adventures* was that we were actually creating a traditional adventure game, and what people

expected from an adventure game, and very honestly what we expected
from an adventure game, changed over the course of the project. And
when we got to the point where we canceled it, it was just because we
looked at where we were and said, you know, this would have been great
three years ago. (Roper)

Roper's explanation focused on the mindset within the company, one
known for its consistent production of industry successes. He does not
acknowledge outright the state of affairs within the industry, in which
the adventure game genre was being pronounced dead. However, he
does imply an evolution of the adventure game genre that could be seen
as death for the classical form. Indeed, *Warcraft Adventures*' screenshots and comic narrative focus resemble genre classics. However, even
though in canceling the project Roper believed that the "adventure game
is still the single best way to tell a story," none of Blizzard's later releases
featured the character-driven narrative suggested by *Warcraft Adventures*'
screenshots and early media. One reading of the cancellation might be
that Blizzard was put off by the low sales of similar titles and perceptions
of the genre's death across the industry, and refused to release a project
that wouldn't meet its usual standards in sales—an unusual decision
given that the game was complete. This attitude reflected a very mainstream approach typical of many of the decisions made in the industry
at the time: even though adventure games might still have an audience,
and several designers believed in their storytelling power, the declining
sales seemed to point toward ignoring that "smaller" market for other
genres with higher sales numbers.

Perhaps in part because of this industry shift, companies did not
see any value in their older adventure game franchises. Many other
projects were closed down, partly finished, as corporations did not
anticipate rewards from completing what had been started. Sequels
were announced, delayed indefinitely, and finally canceled—like the
LucasArts game *Full Throttle II*, which was started in 2000 and abandoned when a quarter complete. Even the abandoned project showed the
attempt to update the lead character for a new market, with screenshots
released showing off enhanced graphics. Perhaps made wary by the
widespread changes across the industry, fans were afraid the new sequel

would move too far from the original gameplay and lack the humor that lead designer Tim Schafer had brought to the first installment (Ratliff and Jong). Fans could see evidence of the ramifications of shifts to 3-D in the transformation of *King's Quest* and *Indiana Jones*, leaving them no reason to trust the continuity of sequels to initial installments in the series. The sequel was revived in 2003 only to be canceled again with a final statement from LucasArts: "We do not want to disappoint the many fans of *Full Throttle*, and hope everyone can understand how committed we are to delivering the best-quality gaming experience that we possibly can" (Ratliff and Jong).

So what "killed" the adventure game? The move to 3-D graphics is certainly a suspect, but the transformation of gaming—and console gaming in particular—into a more and more commercially viable and mainstream industry also takes its share of the blame. The alteration of interfaces from the text-based, narrative exploration of the early text and graphical games to the mouse-hunt for pixels in increasingly familiar 3-D worlds certainly did not help. Finally, the distinctive, deliberately abstract or comic-inspired 2-D graphics of early games, easier to animate and demanding less processing power, were lost briefly in the generic look of early 3-D.

But was the genre really dead? As the adventure game form diminished commercially, *King's Quest* designer Roberta Williams responded to those mourning its death: "If you go back and look at where adventure games were and where they went, you can see that the adventure game is still there, it's just a different/better (depending on your particular point of view) experience playing them. The adventure game 'as we know it' just keeps evolving. It's still evolving" (White). As the woman responsible for the incorporation of graphics to the text-based world of interactive fiction in the first place, Roberta Williams was certainly not one to be threatened by graphical innovations as a potential genre killer. The addition of 3-D graphics does not inherently interfere with the genre's structures fundamentally, as the critical (if not financial) success of *Grim Fandango* confirmed.

Imagine what would be possible if the abandoned code, images, and partial production for a game such as *Full Throttle II* were released to the creative commons for a do-over. What value does this unfinished content have to the company? Clearly, it represents an investment of resources, time, and money, but those resources have yielded nothing marketable. The same possibilities could revitalize *Warcraft Adventures* had Blizzard been willing to cede control of the nearly-finished content: had the company, for instance, tapped into a fan community of creators desperate to be a part of Blizzard, it would have found many willing to try and find the innovation that could once again make the project marketable. Instead, the company released a novelization that filled the same gap in the narration and let the entire game languish in a Blizzard vault (Roper). Of course, hopes of long-term profitability give the creators reason to cling to their intellectual property in anticipation of some future pay-off—a pay-off that for some projects was waiting around the corner, with the shift back toward storytelling that occurred for a section of the industry at the turn of the next decade.

ADVENTURE GAMES PRESERVED

Fans faced with the cancellation and abandonment of their favorite games did more than bemoan their fate: they have taken an active role in preserving and revitalizing the genre. Indeed, much of what remains playable from the history of adventure games owes not to the efforts of companies (or even archivists) but to the intervention of adventure game fan communities. A fan in 2005 could not walk into a gaming store and find even a trace of most classic games beyond the occasional halfhearted release of a legacy collection. Both of the titans of the classic adventure game industry make such occasional nods to the fans of these games: Sierra last released a collection of *King's Quest* games in 2006, while LucasArts released "archive" collections from 1995 to 1998. These collections are nothing more than a careless repackaging of the originals: the *King's Quest* collection even includes the free software that allows the old game to work on a new system, but some configuration and fuss are still necessary, and hardware support for graphics and sound is far from guaranteed. Sierra did not make the effort to restructure the games for modern systems; instead, it relied upon a program that emulates the operating system that was standard during the classic era of adventure games. The program, DoSBox, permits games that relied on the old Sound Blaster cards and limited memory to adapt to newer systems that would otherwise render such games unplayable.

Aside from such classic collections, the adventure games remain under copyright protection, controlled by the companies that developed them but which have moved on to different systems. Even the archives keeping the classic games available are often shut down for legal concerns: copyright law keeps the games under protection even though commercial sales have disappeared. Unlike books, games rarely go back into print for a new run except in the occasional archive collection, in part because the medium of computer games is very forward-looking— there is always new platform on the horizon.

As a result, playing old games on today's computers becomes a quest in itself: not only have advances in hardware led to incompatibility, but the games themselves are hard to acquire. Some gamers preserved the original floppy disks, but floppy drives are no longer a standard component of PCs. Disintegration of old game materials has led to their virtual preservation: fans scan the manuals, convert the graphic novel introductions to digital forms, and so forth, redistributing them with no legal rights to the contents. Games themselves persist through similarly illegal online distribution. In spite of copyright, fans are taking de facto ownership of these titles. These games retain an appeal and audience even in an era in which gaming has left 2-D environments behind in favor of increased graphical realism and elaborate gaming engines. Fans cite the failure of modern games to capture the old spirit of humor and story-driven play as a motive for their efforts, and even they voice the common lament that adventure gaming in the classic sense is dead.

In keeping creative works alive illegally, adventure game fans are participating in the culture of sharing typical of the current moment, a sharing that has not always been in conflict with intellectual property protections. Copyright law was not always about keeping ideas locked away, tethered to an original creator and held in a sacred trust, immune to the revisions of others. To return to Cory Doctorow's description, the true purpose of copyright is to "decentralize who gets to make art" (79). This is an idea that a generation raised on social media can understand implicitly. Everyone is a creator now; everyone is an author. Facebook,

Twitter, MySpace, YouTube, Blogger, LiveJournal—these are familiar hallmarks of digital creativity online. These are places where people create content for no better reason than to share it. These are places for storytelling, whether those stories are told through an assemblage of video clips building a scene or a series of 140-character messages describing a bad day at the DMV. They are places where one rarely stops to think: who owns this? To have your idea ripped off, "retweeted," or remixed is the highest form of flattery, and memes are founded on a mindset of share-and-share alike.

An idea remade or remixed stays relevant—and can be built on. Unlike corporate properties, fan creations are without possessive authors, particularly when the work is so derivative that the fan author cannot even lay claim to it, and so others are free to build upon it. Often fan works begin with acknowledgments of influence, noting that aside from the primary game of influence in the fan work there are other media from both commercial and shared spaces shaping the fan's story. The commercial producers cannot stop their ideas from seeping into shared space nor should they want to, according to Lawrence Lessig:

> The Internet is the age of the hybrid . . . If sharing economies promise value, it is the commercial economy that is tuned to exploit that. But as those in the commercial economy are coming to see, you can't leverage value from a sharing economy with a hostile buyout or a simple acquisition of assets. You have to keep those participating in the sharing economy happy, and for the reasons they were happy before. For here too money can't buy you love, even if love could produce lots of money. (*Remix* 178)

In the realm of games, fan projects presume that when the original producer has ceased to market the original game, it is "abandonware" and therefore available for others to remake. The corporate interests in heritage games oppose this presumption, particularly after the emergence of digital distribution to a range of platforms and the corresponding viability of old titles. Legally, fan remixing and revisiting of content is questionable, if not simply forbidden. The practice of preserving games as abandonware is debated even within the fan community. In a forum thread on the subject, participants went back and forth on the legality and desirability of the practice. The forum's official policy forbids listing links to freeware, but most of the participants argued that the practice of archiving abandonware isn't depriving anyone of income:

> Some game publishers have been good enough to make their old games freeware—such as Revolution recently did with *Beneath a Steel Sky*, but there are several others (notably LucasArts and Sierra) who feel that they would be missing out on a potential money maker by doing so. (Of course, practically speaking they wouldn't get away with selling a collection of old DOS games into a Windows XP marketplace these days, so I'm not sure what hopes they're clinging onto.) If an abandonware case ever came to court, I think it would be very hard for the company to prove that (for example) *Police Quest 1* being on the internet for free download had lost them any revenue, but of course nobody has the time or money to bring a test case to find out. (Pumaman)

Of course, no legal issue of this kind can be settled by public debate, but in this instance the practices of the community are more likely to be influenced by opinion than law. Legal action against abandonware sites, which offer out-of-print games for anyone to download, is possible but rare, and such archives can easily spring up again even after they are challenged.

The most critical concern for many of the players of adventure games, and the independent archivists who gather both the digital and physical ephemera of the gaming industry, is the very real risk of losing a game entirely. Occasionally people post in search of these forgotten games, hoping that someone else took the precaution of saving a copy before it disappeared completely. The Internet Archive, one of the few sites available right now for finding old material, is incomplete and does not offer much in the way of game files of this kind. No entity with the purpose of keeping an absolute archive of these types of stories exists. What do we lose because of this lack of systematic record-keeping? Potentially, the entire history of a genre, and countless stories, could be lost in part because of the same lack of perceived value in preservation that led to the loss of most Hollywood films made prior to 1928 (Pierce 5). Preservation has only recently become a larger conversation within the industry, as the International Game Developers Association white paper on digital game preservation released in 2009 notes: "The question at hand—'What if we do nothing to archive and preserve digital games?'—is spurious: collectively, we (i.e., publishers, players, pundits, and scholars as well as developers) do nothing every day. Rather than collaborate systematically to conserve the cultural and material heritage of our medium, we go about the process of preservation idiosyncratically and haphazardly, if at all" (Lowood et al. 16). Fans are an important part of that tradition of selective preservation.

Perhaps an entire tradition will be reduced to a collection of broken links—this in an age when information is instantly and infinitely reproducible—that's the fear of many adventure game fans. Given the scale of the industry's production and what Lowood and colleagues note as the currently scattered approach to preservation, no one institution or company is likely to be the savior. While physical texts are more actively archived, and libraries have established approaches to keeping up with at least a portion of both printed books and more ephemeral magazines and newspapers, digital archiving is more haphazard. In many ways the members of the *Adventure Game Studio* community have been their own archivists, serving not only as gatekeepers and restorers of classic texts but also as preservers of their own art. This is not an unfamiliar problem for researchers concerned with digital artifacts. As Lawrence Lessig asks, "How is it that we've created a world where researchers trying to understand the effect of media on nineteenth-century America will have an easier time than researchers trying to understand the effect of media on twentieth-century America?" (*Free Culture* 110). Aside from a few independent projects, such as the work of Jason Scott and the Internet Archive, answering this question has been left to the companies that choose to preserve their own legacies—and the fans who choose to do so for them, regardless of the rules laid forth by copyright law.

However, commercial digital distribution services are beginning to play a role. Networks such as Steam (2003) focus primarily on current games but include several classics integrated into their digital distribution and licensing services. The appropriately named Great Old Games (2008) service fills a more specific niche, with a catalog of classic adventure game titles, including many of the Sierra titles under discussion here. However, these are relatively recent additions to corporate-endorsed distribution. Prior to the existence of these sites, the primary way to acquire classic games was through abandonware hubs or communities of game preservationists. These official sites are also limited by the availability of and interest of the copyright holder in their older properties, rather than the interest of fans in playing them. Most games do not receive such attention from commercial services: unless there is a perceived market, restoring the games to a playable state is potentially a loss.

Given the limits of corporate preservation efforts, fans will continue to play a role in preserving old genres like the adventure games. The possibilities of accepting fans as part of the process of both preserving a media universe and extending it beyond its original scope can be glimpsed in a hybrid model common in Japan but only relatively recently visible to Americans. *Doujinshi,* Japanese fan-created comics, are "copycat" comics that move beyond the original in some substantial way. As Lessig describes it, "the artist must make a contribution to the art he copies, by transforming it either subtly or significantly" (*Free Culture* 26). There is no legal system in place for these creators to secure rights, nor do the original copyright holders prosecute these derivative efforts. Perhaps most interestingly, the copyright holders might even be aware that prosecuting such creations would hinder innovation within manga itself: "The manga market accepts these technical violations because they spur the manga market to be more wealthy and productive. Everyone would be worse off if *doujinshi* were banned, so the law does not ban *doujinshi*" (Lessig, *Free Culture* 27). Doctorow sees the phenomenon similarly, noting that "some of these [fan-created] titles dwarf the circulation of the work they pay tribute to, and many of them are sold commercially. Japanese comic publishers know a good thing when they see it, and these fanficcers get left alone by the commercial giants they attach themselves to" (90).

It is hard to imagine a similar system completely taking off in the United States, where a greater number of lawyers exists in part to enforce ownership strictly—ostensibly to preserve creativity. Yet the Japanese system actually lengthens the long tail of art by producing works that rely upon, and thus extend demand for, the original, and events in the boom-and-bust history of adventure games are suggesting that U.S. commercial producers might be learning the same lessons, particularly as current fan supporters have moved titles from obscurity back to commercial viability (as the addition of Kickstarter will later reveal). When corporations and fans collaborate and talk to each other, as when Sierra granted fans permission to make a full-scale sequel to the *King's Quest* series, intellectual property is (however briefly and hesitantly) treated as a commons and not a gated realm. The door is opening slowly to collaboration between the commercial and communal realms. The adventure game fan community gives a glimpse of the possibilities that might open up if that barrier is fully overcome.

CHAPTER 5

Fan Games

"It sounds," Carl said, "as if my friend established a relationship with Nell's copy—"

"And by extension, with Nell," said Lord Finkle-McGraw.

Carl said, "May I inquire as to why you wish to contact the ractor?"

"Because she is a central part of what is going on here," said Lord Finkle-McGraw, "which I did not expect. It was not a part of the original plan that the ractor would be important." (Stephenson 333)

THROUGHOUT THE GOLDEN AGE of the adventure game, the players were essential. In online communities forming around the web, such players were moving from creative play to playful creation. Adventure game fan creators work in a manner that is collaborative and yet personal in the tradition of Don Woods and William Crowthers's *Colossal Cave Adventure*: they build games and tools, share those processes and their code, and expand upon the games and tools made both within the community and outside it in commercial projects. Henry Jenkins has identified this "participatory culture"—in which everyone is active in creating and mediating the culture—as one of the defining aspects of fandom (*Textual Poachers*). Some of this communal, participatory creativity is intertwined with issues of ownership as most fan works violate copyright. However, these authors are not merely continuing the tradition of the "original" games but, importantly, are adding their own ideas. The works in this tradition are a glimpse of the future of electronic literature. These are games created not by so-called independent or corporate collectives but by individuals working within a collective to develop this style of interactive narrative in their own images. Many of the creators might not identify themselves as aspiring to revolutionize electronic literature, yet their patterns of practice resemble those typical of literary salons in their communal support of creativity and collaborative methods, made virtual. In the growing communities that celebrate this form of authorship we can see a narrative tradition growing from early examples, not unlike the stories originally serialized at the birth of the novel. It is here—and in spaces like it, throughout the Internet—where older forms of popular culture are routinely processed, consumed, remediated, and taken as inspiration for new content that holds its audience through a shared heritage of stories taking advantage of the affordances of new media for production and distribution.

Paul Levinson offers the term "new new media" as a way of focusing on the most social of online spaces, envisioning an "empowered new new media user . . . [who] has the option of producing content and consuming content produced by hundreds of millions of other new new media consumer-producers" (4). But the term is misleading, as this type of production has been part of adventure games from the very beginning, and the addition of new social networks has simply made it easier to widely distribute what was already being freely produced and shared. The fan games and tools are part of the ecosystem of "new new" but also are anchored in the communal models of creativity that predate any such label. In these works lurk models for authorship and for navigating the fan-consumer-producer tensions that go beyond copyright to the heart of the value of creative works. Just as Neal Stephenson's Primer has no magic without the "ractor," Miranda, so too would the adventure game genre remain a mostly forgotten commercial form without the intervention of these fans and storytellers. This extends the active involvement of players in making games function: the move from active reader/player to preservationist and author is an expression of the same engagement with the original.

WORKING IN *ADVENTURE GAME STUDIO*

Years after the golden age of adventure games ended, a designer can create a game with a similar interface and structure using what are essentially re-creations of those classic engines. Some of the earliest players who wanted to create games similar to the classic games developed tools for modeling with the traditional engines. Now many of these tools, which offer a graphical interface for adventure game development, are freely available to other noncommercial game creators. The availability of these free tools lowers the barrier to entry for would-be creators, because the tools eliminate the need for real programming skill. They are, like the games themselves, essentially point and click; even animating sprites is an easy task. Tools of this kind allow for fan game production in much the same way that digital technologies made fan filmmaking easier, as Henry Jenkins has noted: "Digital technologies have also enabled new forms of fan cultural production. . . . Fan filmmakers have used home computers to duplicate effects Lucasfilm had spent a fortune to achieve several decades earlier; many fan films create their own light saber or space battles" (Jenkins, *Fans, Bloggers, and Gamers* 143–144). The online distribution of these tools is crucial to their influence. Would-be creators moved by this particular style of game can easily locate both the tools and the specific tool sets inspired by interfaces of the era; even the most specific of interfaces are often available for easy reproduction, with fans posting tools for creating everything from the LucasArts SCUMM engine to the *Gabriel Knight* (1993, Mac/PC) "talking heads" chat.

Several of the tools available online are based upon the subset of games most often revisited by fan authors: the Sierra and LucasArts games of the 1980s and 1990s. When these classic adventure games were created, the companies had to build the game engines from scratch. They learned and derived much from the text-based interactive fiction games that preceded graphical adventure games, but modeling an interactive graphical environment was then new. The focus on players' interaction with the game environment required designers to take the traditional verbs of text interactions—push, pull, open, take, talk to, and so forth—and revise them to create avatar-based play. The LucasArts SCUMM engine and Sierra's similar engines were proprietary, but the interactive results of their mechanisms were quite visible, and reconstructing those foundations—rather than trying to develop a new 3-D graphics-powered environment—proved to be a manageable challenge for small development teams. Once such team had re-created the game platform as an accessible tool; anyone could pick it up and use it to re-create the affordances of the genre.

Fans have made several different tools available. Of these, the most popular is *Adventure Game Studio*, or *AGS*, a tool for creating games in the classic Sierra style. The first version was released in 1997 for early Windows PCs and relies upon the now-familiar graphical menu style of the era. The most recent version, 3.2.1, was released in April 2011. Taking a closer look at its workings, *AGS* stands out as a highly accessible platform for making games, with a visual user interface not unlike a graphics program. The interface for *AGS* is shown below, here with the graphical interface overlay for managing dialogue options with non-player characters. The interface allows creators to manage all the standard elements of an adventure game with simple code. For example, the script for the game's response to a player looking at a bookshelf might be written:

```
function hBookshelf_Look{}
{
Display("You stop for a moment to examine the bookshelf and scan its
many titles. You spot a zombie apocalypse handbook that may come in
handy . . .");
cSelf.AddInventory(iZombieHandbook);
    }
```

This simple script responds when a player looks at a hotspot (an area of the image that has been labeled by the designer as hBookshelf) with text relevant to the character's current situation and adds an inventory object to the player's resources. Because the software provides the engine model, drawn from the example of the genre's traditions, most of the mechanics are implemented without additional coding—both hotspot and inventory object can be built in the visual editor first, as shown in figure 3. In this version of *Adventure Game Studio* (3.2.1), walkable areas are highlighted in blue, and rooms and objects are managed through an internal file structure.

Beyond providing a graphical interface for game production, *AGS* provides a community: would-be creators put their efforts online for their fellow enthusiasts to download and comment upon. The central hub of *AGS* is an active forum where authors find collaborators with

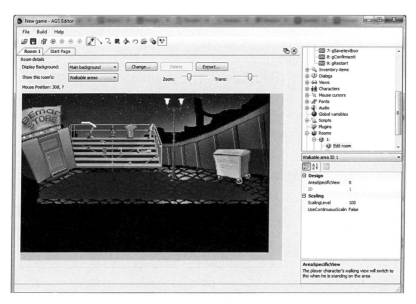

3. *Adventure Game Studio*, editing interface. Version 3.2.1: 2013.

different skill sets, seek out beta testers and advice on construction, and talk about games in general. The community frowns on the production of games for sale, although commercial distribution is possible. Creators are supposed to be motivated by pure love of the game, and perhaps by the desire to create a portfolio that will entice companies to hire them; the standards of this fan community insist on the importance of passion. Furthermore, it is important to note that the creators of these games often play other fans' titles. Playing and creating these games are the mutual rewards of belonging to this community.

In this, the fan authors have much in common with the modders of first-person shooters, whose work similarly rarely provides them with financial rewards even though they create content. Their efforts are distinguished from the more accepted practices of modders (whose work relies on the original game to be playable) or players who build new levels and content for games (called level producers) by their intentions and product. The relationship of the work of modders with the commercial product means that their work distinctively adds to the value of the original game: while it is fan activity, it is also labor that serves the game's creators: "The precarious status of modding as a form of unpaid labour is veiled by the perception of modding as a leisure activity, or simply as an extension of play. This draws attention to the fact that in the entertainment industries, the relationship between work and play is changing, leading, as it were, to a hybrid form of 'playbour'" (Kücklich). Fans ascribe a purity to noncommercial intent that is itself illusory but appealing: the mystique of the fan author driven only by passion rests on the assumption that purity of purpose will protect him or her against accusations of copyright infringement and intellectual property theft. In reality, what fan authors are more likely to achieve is recognition from a community, as games created in this way are eligible for awards given out by the community itself or may be reviewed by one of the websites devoted to the adventure game genre.

Modders build on the original game, melding their efforts with those of the original developers and extending the content in a way that benefits the original copyright holder: "multiplayer FPS [first-person shooter] games are 'co-creative media'; neither developers nor player-creators can be solely responsible for production of the final assemblage regarded as 'the game,' it requires the input of both" (Morris 8). The player-creators that Morris describes actively create new content in the same way as the fan authors of the adventure game community, but the companies that own the first-person shooter games in question have embraced the practice. The developers rely upon the content created by modders to continue to expand playability options within their game and are secure in the knowledge that no one can use these mods without having purchased the original copyrighted games. Fan creators of the classic adventure game movement can also be identified as cocreators, since they are in dialogue with the work of the original developers. The crucial distinction between fan authors in the adventure game community and modders in the first-person shooter community is that the fan authors are not endorsed by those developers. The reason why is simple: fan authors co-opt material from the existing games to create experiences that do not require players to own the original game. A game authored by a fan stands on its own and is playable as a complete structure. It is informed by the original, and may even be an exacting remake of the original, but it is developed separately. While the work of modders is tied to the original game by a web of interdependence, the games created by fan authors can even go so far as to replace the original game and render ownership of it irrelevant. The patterns of production in these two genres show the transfer of creative control from the original corporate authors to fans. The heritage of adventure games both in particular titles and in the general form has become a playground for new content creation. Game making as a cultural production does not belong to corporations, and the center of innovation is quickly moving to these outer circles, though under somewhat different circumstances depending on the genre.

Like modders, the new cocreators of these "neoclassic" adventure games are fusing play and labor. They produce content without reimbursement for their time or efforts. In turn, they make that content freely available, easily downloadable by fellow enthusiasts through communal hubs like the *AGS* website. Sometimes these releases are even in clear competition with the commercial endeavors of the primary creators, as with the *King's Quest* remakes and Sierra's re-release of the series. However, this competition goes mostly ignored—the remakes belong to one world while the re-releases occupy another. This is best understood as a symptom of Lessig's notion of the hybrid economy, in which distinctions are maintained between an economy of "sharing" and an economy of "commerce" (*Remix* 177). In the perception and communities of fans, remakes build the value of the games, keeping them alive and active, even if the audience is small. Fans gain status within their community for the value of the works they've authored, and most fan communities reward authors with attention and feedback—the currency of an economy of sharing. Corporate game producers, on the other hand, are more concerned with ownership: while authorship may have passed to the fans, ownership remains in the hands of the creators. Were the fan creators to try to profit from their remakes, they would no longer be operating in the spirit of sharing and would present a clearer threat to the commercial value of the brand.

Yet despite the lack of monetary rewards, fan cocreators persist and through their authorship continually re-create the worlds of their devotion through a still-evolving tradition of folk art gone digital. The term "folk art" is perhaps most appropriate because many producers strive within a tradition, not in the direct wake of a particular work: fan games are only one form of *AGS* activity, as many more games are made following the aesthetics of adventure games with 2-D graphics, puzzle solving, and narrative. Thus many of the works appear similar, yet "textual and visual reproduction on the Internet does not necessarily homogenize cultural expression" (Bronner 35). There is diversity in emergent game structures, even within the adventure game tradition. This continues the metaphor of folk art, which relies on individual production within traditions that no one person "owns."

Members of the *Adventure Game Studio* community are often, if not always, of an age to have grown up with adventure games—rather like myself. The *AGS* community noted in a self-study in March 2004 that "the actual average age on the forums at present is 22 years old. There is, of course, a reason for the majority age group being young adults— people that are aged about 20 now would have played games like *Monkey Island* and *King's Quest* when they were children, and are now old enough to want to re-create the games" (AGS). This self-description acknowledges the impact the classic games have made and continue to make on the *AGS* productions, which are themselves created with an interface designed to allow work expanding upon the tradition. Fan authors continually evoke the games of the classical era of the genre, both in completely new games with original narratives, graphics, and puzzles and in re-releases, remastering, and extensions of the classic universes.

Just as the players of adventure games were historically unlike the majority of other gamers, the fan authors in this genre differ from modders. Adventure games are linked with casual games, which Jesper Juul defines as accessible and often associated with positive fiction, ease of entry, and simple mechanics (*Angry Birds* and *Bejeweled* are two notable examples). Juul observed the connection between *Myst* (1993, Mac— ported to Sega Saturn, Windows, PlayStation, etc.) and the casual game revolution, and noted that among baby boomers, *Myst* is "the most common first computer game played, as well as the most common favorite computer game" (*Casual Revolution* 27). This experience helps differentiate adventure game fans from the stereotypical gamer community, as adventure games have never been part of the "hardcore" gaming realm. Even *Myst* has experienced a recent resurgence, with a release on the iPhone boasting graphics identical to the original. This transition onto a new platform allows *Myst* to recapture its original audience, now owners of smartphones and tablets, which are ideal for short game experiences that can be picked up and put down again quickly. These new devices offer a fitting platform for one of the great adventure games in the recent mainstreaming of interactive storytelling, particularly given the role *Myst* played in widening the potential audience of the genre with its original release.

Jesper Juul notes the demographic overlaps between the *Myst* audience and today's casual game players: "Games like *Myst, Monopoly*, and *Lego Island*—also three of the most popular computer games of 1997—appeal to a much broader audience of males and females of all ages that want easy-to-learn family games. These games tend to use simple technology, and sell steadily year after year" (*Casual Revolution* 26). Some of this diversity is reflected in the *AGS* community, which had already formed when games like *Myst* introduced adventure games to a wider audience and started to shape the demographics of casual games. Such demographics do not much resemble the popular image of serious gamers as teenage males, and are thus particularly valuable in also transforming our vision of who makes games. Designer and critic Anna Anthropy has observed the power of gaming-developing communities such as "Glorious Trainwrecks," which encourages the "true spirit of indie gaming" by rejecting "production values" in favor of amateur creativity (Glorious Trainwrecks). As Anthropy observed, one of the most powerful roles for tools like *AGS* is in widening the range of producers of games. She advocates for highly personal production in games:

> What I want from videogames is a plurality of voices. I want games to come from a wider set of experiences and present a wider range of perspectives. I can imagine—you are invited to imagine with me—a world in which digital games are not manufactured by publishers for the same small audience, but one in which games are authored by you and me for the benefit of our peers. (Anthropy 8)

The industry often (incorrectly) carries assumptions about the demographics of game players to the creators of those same games, but platforms like *Adventure Game Studio* make it increasingly possible for anyone (particularly those from marginalized or underrepresented groups within the gaming-development community) to engage in interactive storytelling and game-making. While commercial games such as *Myst* are key inspirations for the *AGS* community, the studio itself is founded on free creation and free content. In adopting this stance, the community is part of a larger trend online, what David Bollier terms the "viral spiral." He is describing the seemingly chaotic process of social creation centered on programs just like *AGS*: "The viral spiral began with free software (code that is free to use, not code at no cost) and later produced the web. Once these open platforms had sufficiently matured, tech wizards realized that software's great promise is not as a stand-alone tool on PCs, but as a social platform for web-based sharing and collaboration" (Bollier 3).

AGS is only one of the many game-creation platforms; however, of such tools it is one of the more accessible and customized to the following of the adventure game tradition while still allowing advanced users flexibility. This lends itself to the formation of a community that shares common origin texts (a folk art tradition). The revolution in content creation that has accompanied the move to digital distribution begins with the model of free creation. The games under analysis here were heirs to commercial products but are not themselves inherently commercial—in fact, most are released with no more expectation than to reach a limited player base that mostly consists of other game creators of the same genre. This noncommercial form puts narrative and expression ahead of technological advancement, because creating a game in the modern style requires substantial capital and a large team with varying expertise. The new creators of interactive narrative content in this noncommercial tradition are not faced with the same challenges as the producers of the classic games, who needed to create game engines to handle the interactions they envisioned. The communities themselves have built and freely shared tools— such as *Adventure Game Studio*, *SLUDGE*, and *AGI Studio*—that transform the process of creation into something manageable by an individual author. Similar tools include *Twine*, a free hypertext game-creation tool; *Inform 7*, a natural language processing tool for building interactive fiction; and *Game Maker*, a broad platform for game development with a commercial version. Its user-friendliness allows *AGS* to play a significant role in the viral spiral, in which freely created content, both in the form of tools and narratives, inspires further creation and cycles through the community. Works produced using *AGS* tools occasionally appear alongside commercial releases on reviewing sites dedicated to the adventure game genre. Players are more willing to pick up games reviewed in this manner because they're free, and would-be creators are not barred from the process by the expense of the tools. This community serves as a space for recognition of authors and promotion of content, broadening the reach in the larger spaces of adventure game fans.

I first came to observe *AGS* as a community through its role as an archive and gatekeeper for the not-all-forgotten adventure games of the classic era. Its members include fans, but a distinctive type of fan: their allegiance is to the genre of adventure games, not to specific games. And their community is built around fan authorship. Members have built remakes of several classics using the *AGS* tools, and while the community itself opposes links to illegal abandonware and blocks them, there is no similar feeling against the works of fan player-creators. The investment of time by those creators is enough to create a sense of ownership by individual authors of their works when distributed among the community, even in the case of fan works that owe a clear debt to commercial games.

FANS AS PRODUCERS

Putting *AGS* into the larger context of fan productions requires first recognizing what makes the *AGS* community unique. Over my two years observing the community, I noticed three phenomena:

> 1. The *AGS* fan movement has sustained itself for a decade developing narrative games in parallel to and in conversation with the mainstream gaming industry.
> 2. Although similar types of fan production have attracted the attention of studies of transformative works and participatory culture, this particular fandom has gone largely ignored—in part, perhaps, because while

other fandoms focus on clearly identifiable media artifacts, this fandom focuses on a narrative style.

 3. While our understanding of the storytelling potential of games has often focused on mainstream titles, communities such as that surrounding *AGS* often bring clearly narrative intentions to their interactive work. Placing this type of project within the evolution of interactive storytelling fills an important gap in explaining how this genre has reached its current status.

The mainstream sequels are not the real heirs to the literary aspirations of the original games: that legacy belongs to the players turned creators working in online communities to create games in the tradition of the classics but with their own visions fully embodied in the style of the genre. The video games of today are often left outside the gates of electronic literature, regarded as pulp fiction cousins to the more serious hypertextual and nonlinear experiments. Conversely, the most gamelike experiments within electronic literature might be given the label of "serious games" or held as extremes of what the form can produce rather than as evidence of its capacity to generate meaning through interactivity. Yet the games produced as heirs to the adventure game genre offer one vision for the future of literature in a digital age when ideas can move freely from commercial to communal space, and the fact that they have gone largely ignored needs to be remedied to understand the role these narratives are still playing in our culture—particularly as creators emerge from these communities of practice and turn their attention to new platforms where such forms are no longer being marginalized.

 As noted above, the *AGS* fandom and similar communities have sustained themselves for a couple of decades while going largely unnoticed, creating games in parallel to the commercial firms. At first, fan production seems to be innovation that builds on corporate-produced games, while corporate games remain on their own path of evolution. Attention to fan production in other mediums, particularly in the writing of fanfiction and creation of fan films building on television and film, demonstrates that a back and forth between fan and corporate producer is possible and common. Remix culture influences the mobility of ideas within and beyond a community: "Remixes happen within a community of remixers. In the digital age, that community can be spread around the world . . . They are showing one another how they can create. . . . That showing is valuable, even when the stuff produced is not" (Lessig, *Remix* 77). Corporations are not immune to this influence: if we extend Lessig's vision of the community of remixers, all creators of content (commercial and fan) share in showing and learning. Noncommercial endeavors can take more risks in production, and while the community puts a strong value on good games, with awards every year recognizing achievement, it also rewards participation regardless of the quality of the final output. Lessig's point—that the action is more valuable than the output—thus applies, although in this case the experimental and educational nature of the process of creative activity is part of what ensures future creativity, with boundary-pushing games valued as much as those that echo their predecessors in form or gameplay. Members of the community play both commercial games and fan games, and while it appears that only other fans play fan-created games, the line between creator and fan is blurry if it exists at all. Current trends in production suggest that the movement between (and coidentification) of fan and designer is common. Given that: What is the power of *Adventure Game Studio*? Can the output of this type of creative activity go beyond "niche" market games to influence the course of interactive storytelling?

Adventure Game Studio enables distributed game authorship, and the quality of works produced varies accordingly—no one game foretells the future of interactive storytelling. Online space is filled with creators who build things despite knowing that someone else's might be "better." Although Lessig contended that among remix practitioners, sharing their works is more important than attaining a certain level of quality, that need not to be taken as a dismissal of the works of the sharing economy. Instead, it is something to celebrate: not every fan game need break out of the conventional format or give voice to a story not normally heard within the space of interactive narrative; at the same time, the ease of entry into this realm makes works that do deviate from the mainstream in these ways possible. The freedom to imagine, without the pressure of marketability, allows a form to evolve. Personal adventure games are but one form to emerge from the remix, but they offer a hybrid of traditional storytelling and interactive media that stands as a bastion of folk creativity in the hybrid economy. Even as commercial culture moves on, and the boundaries between commercial and sharing are renegotiated to acknowledge the demands of a generation that expects to freely consume, remix, and create culture with equal freedom, fans of adventure games will be preserving and expanding a canon of stories that will not be surrendered to the black hole of obsolescence.

The type of authorship that the early adventure games required from players was more metaphorical than literal. Players did not write any of the text, and while their emotional investment was required for the power of the narrative, it was not required for its execution. Now players are literally being transformed into authors. Creators today are emerging from the first generation to grow up with video games embedded in their early experience, and this state—the state of the so-called digital native—allows for a different approach to the process of creation. Previous game creators were shaping the form from the influences of traditional narratives—the games they created were necessarily compared with literature and film because these were the models available for both inspiration and contemporary parallels.

The blurring of the positions of reader and author is happening everywhere on the web. Posters on YouTube remix, imitate, and innovate in short video postings that can respond to one another in linked webs of dialogue. Fan works keep a series long "dead" in the hands of its producers alive—witness the large communities around chronologically colocated franchises *Harry Potter* (1997–2007, print), *Buffy the Vampire Slayer* (1997–2003, television), and even the many series of *Star Trek* (1966–2005, television). Players of massive multiplayer games become cocreators of the game experience, building their characters and creating the social networks and add-ons that make the game a lasting world. It is tempting to see adventure game creators as just one more node in this growing culture of cocreation. However, the games made by *AGS* community members only occasionally build upon artifacts from the original commercial games, which is a more common practice in other fan communities. More often, *AGS* members remember the original, but are concerned with shaping the new.

This type of practice is growing across gaming and interactive production, and it is this movement of playful creation that *AGS* exemplifies.

PLATE 1. *Maniac Mansion*. Lucasfilm Games, 1987.

PLATE 2. *Myst*. Cyan, 1993.

PLATE 3. *King's Quest IV: The Perils of Rosella*. Sierra Entertainment, 1988.

PLATE 4. *Warcraft Adventures* (unreleased). Blizzard, intended 1997.

PLATE 5. *The Night of the Meteor* (unreleased, working screenshot). Edison Interactive, 2013.

PLATE 6. *King's Quest II: Romancing the Stones* (fan remake). AGDI, 2002.

PLATE 7. *Adventure: The Inside Job*. Akril, 2008.

PLATE 8. *Out of Order*. Hungry Software, 2008.

PLATE 9. *Cirque de Zale*. Kinoko, 2004.

PLATE 10. *What Linus Bruckman Sees When His Eyes Are Closed*. Vince Twelve, 2006.

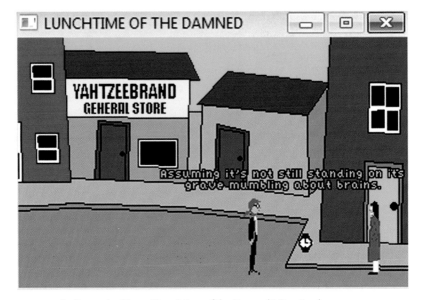

PLATE 11. Reality-on-the-Norm: "Lunchtime of the Damned." Ben Croshaw. 2001.

PLATE 12. *The Silver Lining Episode 1: What Is Decreed Must Be*. Phoenix Online Studios, 2010.

PLATE 13. *Zack and Wiki: Quest for Barbaros' Treasure.* Capcom, 2007.

PLATE 14. *Leisure Suit Larry Reloaded.* Replay Games, 2013.

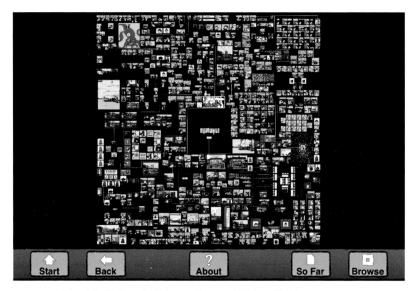

PLATE 15. *Meanwhile* (iOS version). Jason Shiga and Andrew Plotkin, 2012.

PLATE 16. *Lucy and Lola's Big Adventure*. Jane Jensen, Pinkerton Road Studio. 2013.

Playful transformative works can be seen in the interactive fiction community, as with Flourish Klink's interactive fiction piece *Muggle Studies* (2012, Inform 7), a commentary on exclusion and marginalized voices and characters within the Harry Potter universe delivered as an interactive story from the viewpoint of a newly hired lesbian Muggle Studies teacher on her first day at Hogwarts. The implicit prejudices of the Hogwarts' tiered universe, where life as a wizard of a certain kind is much more desirable than the life of a muggle or nonmagic user, are explored and parodied in contrast to the same inequalities in our own society (Klink). The piece is successful as social satire but also uses the form of interactive fiction to make the player part of the studied society. The work is particularly poignant when compared to other "games" in the *Harry Potter* universe from officially sanctioned production, such as the *Lego Harry Potter* (2010, consoles and computers) series and *Pottermore* (2011, online game), which we return to when we visit the world of "magical books." The official games are primarily escapist: they represent Hogwarts while offering a further glimpse of the author's world, but without critiquing or revealing anything further about the assumptions behind the narrative. This type of project is a reminder that it is possible to visit certain stories and worlds meaningfully through interactive platforms, despite what commercial releases might suggest—it is simply that they haven't commonly been explored through an intentionally framed combination of media.

In the case of *Muggle Studies*, the story is powered by *Inform 7*—another communal creative tool designed for accessibility, as previously noted for its resemblance to *AGS*. *Inform 7* is particularly accessible to writers because the "grammar" of the programming language echoes that of English. But while the interactive fiction community is clearly associated with literary forms, and keeps its ties to textuality intact from its roots in Infocom and other classics, amateur graphical adventures are more inherently removed from such consideration by their greater perceived distance from the traditionally literary. The communities share common early influences in gamebooks and Crowther's *Colossal Cave Adventure*, and similarly benefit from the availability of a platform for the community to build on and with.

Some tropes, such as the one-room game, are common to both the

AGS and *Inform 7* communities. The hobbyist is most likely to be able to complete a game that is confined in scope to a reasonable scale—given the availability of time to shape the world—and both interactive fiction and graphic adventure games share a number of single room exemplars. Some games, like Andrew Plotkin's previously mentioned *Shade*, break the expectations of the single room by taking the player deeper into psychological space, relationships with time, or even other experimentation with literary devices. In *Adventure Game Studio*, there is a similar refuge in the single screen for first-time game makers, with the disadvantage that the concreteness of a graphic image limits the potential depth of a displayed room to what the screen can reasonably hold. I could thus note that the addition of graphics makes storytelling that transcends the spatial constraints of the screen more challenging—but to make that assertion boldly would be to embrace the same flawed logic that caused publishers to abandon the adventure game genre wholesale when 3-D graphics seemed to push the genre into irrelevance. Instead, I argue that examining the output of this type of creative community reveals storytelling forms that embrace both graphics and text alongside interactivity.

There are a few aspects that make the *AGS* community a good microcosm for considering the future of cocreative work. As the community has existed for over a decade, continually unified by one main forum and software tool, it is easily defined in its age and scale. While other software tools exist for creating adventure games, none has built the type of presence that *AGS* has. The community remains in a state of production throughout all seasons, with new members coming and going and projects posted regularly throughout the year. Some are elaborate games, some single-room affairs without much content, but nearly all are made freely available and commented upon by others. The community encourages and hosts these works, allowing a better grasp of the range of content. Obviously some projects in this genre remain private and impossible to track, while others are never completed or published, but a large archive does exist, and it includes most of the work created with *AGS* tools.

The forums are continually active: this is not a dead community even though many of the games that inspired its existence are now unplayable on modern systems. Fans are continually fighting the forces of obsolescence, returning games to a playable state through a number of methods I examine in the following pages. David Bollier's "viral spiral" continues as games are played by and inspire fans, which in turn leads to evolution within the creation tools themselves. This is crucial: the production tools did not remain stagnant once sufficient resources were available to re-create what the genre was known for producing; instead, the authorial toolset has continued to grow, and some creators have built their own extensions to address gaps, just as creators within the *Inform 7* community have added new "vocabulary" to *Inform 7* through their own libraries. The conversation is always going. Each year the community puts its best games up to a vote by community members and awards the best produced—and despite the age of the system, there are always new games to vote on. In 2012, the winners for 2011 included both innovative original games and remakes such as *King's Quest III*, which was voted as better than the original—a reminder both of how long it's been and how valued the classic games still are within the community, that such attention to a reproduction is warranted.

Despite this apparently harmonious model, some suspicion of an open-source, creative-commons world even exists within the community itself: the creator of *Adventure Game Studio*, Chris Jones, once refused to release the source code. He cited his fears that to do so would not only allow others to turn his code toward personal commercial ends but also allow other people to more easily reverse-engineer others' games (AGS). This decision in some ways limited the potential of the software, but the ease of adding modular content and creating "expansion packs" for the original toolset allowed innovation to continue. However, the *Adventure Game Studio* codebase was released in 2011, allowing for forked projects such as the SkyGoblin branch to add support for new features, such as custom resolution and other graphics options (SkyGoblin [Markus]).

The tension between creativity and ownership is hardly new and has helped to shape the *AGS* community. Games in the archive are credited, and if a creator has a strong reputation, his or her releases may even lead to donations or paid sales. The rebirth of adventure games as a commercial genre, which I examine in chapter 7, suggests new viability for *AGS* games in the market, and a commercial-fan tension exists alongside the realization of player-creators that their own work might have a potential paying audience.

Examining personal interactive narrative projects outside of the corporate frameworks demonstrates the vitality of a folk art tradition. A study of the games produced within the community reveals the different facets of these creations. Particularly interesting is the creation of an internal heritage network: a series of games, based on an original collaborative creation, that continues to build on a canon produced within the community. These projects, even when created by an individual, reveal a shared world in which the fan-creations in turn spawn more creation, and individual productions take the place of corporate productions at the center of a network. Most important, the games I examine draw attention to the potential of this form to innovate in areas that the commercial world is less likely to value.

FAN REMAKES

One of the classic adventure games mentioned previously, *Maniac Mansion*, languishes in the LucasArts vault. It was last released as a playable application on a computer within its own sequel, *Day of the Tentacle*. That version was riddled with bugs: launching the game often crashed the system if its hardware was too advanced. A German enthusiast, known online as LucasFan, put in hours converting the game to *Maniac Mansion Deluxe* (2004, *AGS*), a freely available and improved version of the original *Maniac Mansion*. LucasFan created the game using *Adventure Game Studio* to input the old environments and model anew the avatars and characters. Unlike the old version, which was constructed for the DOS operating system, this new version is playable on a range of computers and has in effect archived the *Maniac Mansion* experience for gamers present and future. Despite the decision by Sierra to release *Mystery House* to the public domain and open the door for projects like "Mystery House Taken Over," most adventure games—including *Maniac Mansion*—remained under copyright. LucasFan earned an endorsement from the game's creator, but not from its copyright holders at LucasArts: "I think it's incredible," said *Maniac Mansion* cocreator David Fox. "When we first released these games, we figured people would be interested for two or three years, max. The fact people still care enough to put this kind of work into the games, it's amazing" (Ogles). David Fox can be credited with recognizing his own work as part of a tradition of folk art. He accepts and invites the extension of his creation: to him, the story of *Maniac Mansion* did not end when his creative team shut the final door and put it in a box to ship. However, David Fox could not speak for the company.

LucasFan made several enhancements to the original game for his or her remake. LucasFan incorporated the interface from *Maniac Mansion*'s sequel, *Day of the Tentacle*, and enhanced the graphics. LucasFan also included an easy interface for transitioning among the playable characters and enhanced the verb recognition. In the original version, as seen in plate 1, the spirit of the game is preserved while the quality is enhanced, though not so dramatically as to lose any of the game's original styling. The game now reaches the levels of graphic quality observed in the LucasArts sequel, a quality that was not yet possible when *Maniac Mansion* was originally produced and the SCUMM engine that powers LucasArts classic games was only first developed.

While fellow fans heaped their praises upon LucasFan's efforts, the copyright holders did not view them so kindly. In 2005, LucasFan made a dramatic disappearance from the Internet following rumors of a heated exchange between him or her and the attorneys responsible for LucasArts's cease-and-desist orders. At the time, LucasFan was rumored to be working on an *Indiana Jones* game in the spirit of the original *Indiana Jones and the Fate of Atlantis* adventure game, a project that might have brought him negative attention, given that the *Indiana Jones* license is still profitable for LucasArts (Barwood and Falstein). Details are difficult to confirm because the involved parties were mostly silent on the matter. The LucasFan website notes only: "Recent events have forced us to shut down our web appearance. We would like to thank all our fans and supporters who believed in us and our dreams" (LucasFan). The accompanying image recalls the *Maniac Mansion* remake with a tombstone set outside the famed mansion. The game, however, lives on, and the remake can still be downloaded through new sources that preserve the work. LucasFan as the author is unnecessary for the game's survival now that it is in the hands of a larger community: LucasFan's *Maniac Mansion Deluxe*, which had disappeared from most sites in wake of the legal dispute, still lingers on the web through his last parting message.

While remastering a game for a new system becomes a form of preservation, often one that the game's owner has chosen not to complete, it is also out of the remake author's hands to determine the new game's fate and accessibility.

The rebuilding (or taking over) of *Maniac Mansion* continues as another team calling itself "Edison Interactive" has released a trailer and screenshots for its planned remake *Night of the Meteor* (not yet released, *AGS*). The team has no legal right to produce the game, but as of yet has not been asked to shut down the project. The Edison Interactive introduction evokes the original, despite the change of title, by mentioning key characters such as nurse Edna Edison and her husband and son along with the original meteor crash that started the events of *Maniac Mansion*:

> "Ah! An unwelcome visitor! How silly of me, I should have tied you to my bed!"
> That's how Edna Edison (a nurse who's as nasty as she is ugly) used to greet the male visitors, which were unmindful enough to enter the old Victorian mansion, built on the outskirts of town, where a meteor has crashed over 20 years ago. Nothing has changed since then. Her husband, Dr. Fred, still wasn't at dinner for the past five years and their son, Weird Ed, a paramilitary nut is still waiting for his commando package. So, every time when you play this game, it'll be **The Night of the Meteor!** (Edison Interactive)

Whether this project will ever be completed is unknown (particularly given the purchase of LucasArts and all its games by Disney as of 2012), but the initial screenshots (as seen in plate 5) promise a complete revamp of interface and graphics, powered by *Adventure Game Studio* and recalling *Day of the Tentacle*'s verb-based choice system with a visual inventory.

RETELLING *KING'S QUEST*

As the rights to its games exchanged hands repeatedly, and few collections were ever re-released, Sierra games are unsurprisingly at the center of active fan remastering and restoration efforts. One team, Anonymous Game Developers Interactive (AGDI, formerly known as Tierra), remade the first several games of *King's Quest*. The first remake, *King's Quest I* (2001, *AGS*), served primarily to improve playability. The graphics were improved, the sound and dialogue were increased, and the environments were enhanced, but otherwise these elements generally retained the spirit of the original game. Even after the enhancements, the first game is dated by comparison to later entries in the series. The most impressive aspect of the *King's Quest I* remake was the involvement of the original voice actor responsible for Sir Graham's voice in *King's Quest IV* and *King's Quest V*. As the actor explained in an interview, he was pleased to reprise the role: "For one, doing voices is just plain fun, and I especially enjoy doing them for games. For another, I think that the . . . remake is a great tribute to the original *KQ* series. And, lastly, because I was extremely flattered that they asked me to participate" (Wells). The remake is thus even more in sync with the original games because it has this audio connection through a voice that players of the sequels were already attached to. This continuity gives legitimacy to the project it would otherwise lack: having the original voice of Sir Graham is more authentic than taking a volunteer from the fan community itself.

This first remake was a testament to the potential of AGDI, and it paved the way for more dramatic undertakings. AGDI's next project was to take a dated prequel and utterly reshape its character. The team thus followed its initial effort with a remake of *King's Quest II* that was far more ambitious, intending to fill in gaps in the original plotline, deepen character backgrounds, and generally overhaul the entire experience. The result was a game very different from the original project, even featuring a full voice-over when the original version had no spoken dialogue, only text boxes. The enhancement in this case (as seen in plate 6) is stunning: the game cannot easily be dismissed as a repackaging and is a full remake, rendering settings like the shore with an extended color palette, detail, and moving water. In AGDI's hands, *King's Quest II* becomes a different game from a later decade. AGDI made use of much of what Sierra provided in sequels for imagery and interface but updated the game in its own style. The most recent AGDI *King's Quest* project, *King's Quest III: To Heir Is Human Redux* (2011, *AGS*), bears the moniker *"Redux"* because of the team's ambition to offer a "different interpretation to a familiar story," complete with voice acting and new background environments (AGDI).

The successes of AGDI provide examples of an independently negotiated consensus on the creative commons. Many classic games have little commercial value without intervention—they are unplayable on modern hardware and operating systems and often out-of-date in appearance and interface. The first of these problems can render them completely inaccessible; the latter can simply make them of interest only to a limited audience. The efforts of fans keep files available and build the tools, archives, and guides that make the games playable. The corporations, on the other hand, are doing a poor job of building those same elements around their own properties. The result is that fan remakes are more playable than the originals, as the games will run on more modern systems and can be made available through a simple downloadable executable.

A number of classic games have been remade by fans and brought back to the attention of players new and old. Some are merely repackaged with enhanced graphics and interface; others are fully reworked, with fans trying to patch up holes in the original plot or provide music and voice acting where there was originally only static and text. Who is the true author of a fan remake? Certainly the original designer retains the credit for creating a world worth remastering. As for the fans, they are often hesitant to take any credit at all: consider AGDI's decision to call the team "Anonymous," although its members have in fact made their names public. Yet anonymity is not a protection from accusations of copyright violations, nor does operating anonymously exempt the fan from the murky territory of shared authorship. This is perhaps best understood as a practice that extends Aarseth's consideration of the adventure game genre as folk art, as referenced earlier: works are put into the communal tradition, and new works emerge that continue and expand upon that tradition (Aarseth, "Playing Research" 100). Who is the ultimate author of the game? All the creators involved in the practice. There need be no notion of one auteur, of one author working alone to create a masterpiece. This alternative model rejects the impositions of corporate control and traditional copyright, but it can officially be shut down by copyright owners at any time.

FAN SEQUELS

A fan game that acts as a sequel or a revisioning of a classic adventure game is more likely to be played than an amateur effort without that grounding, although both kinds of works are acts of fandom relative to the genre itself. Such works fit broadly into the category of fanfiction, a contested battleground of fan-created stories that extend or rewrite an original universe. This form reflects what Henry Jenkins describes as the nature of fans as an audience "that refuses to simply accept what they are given, but rather insists on the right to become full participants" (*Convergence Culture* 131). The idea of writing inspired by other stories that have already gained a place in popular mythology is by no means limited to the works labeled as fanfiction found on the web; examples of the same process abound and often achieve great success. One example of this practice is Gregory Maguire's *Wicked* (1995), which takes the rather one-dimensional villainess from *The Wonderful Wizard of Oz* and grants her a full biography, from birth to death. The devices Maguire employs are those of fan authorship, taking a classic work and adding a personal vision—creating new romantic attachments, giving a favorite character new motivation and spark, incorporating influences from more recent political and social concerns. Would the work be as successful if it had not been a work of fanfiction but had instead featured an unknown witch of no particular narrative heritage? It is impossible to be certain, but one thing is clear: as a work of fanfiction, it was instead morphed into a well-received Broadway musical, a distinction few novels, and certainly few works of fan authors, are awarded.

Many fan game sequels adopt the concept of fanfiction but preserve the original medium of the playable story. The LucasArts game *Zak McKracken and the Alien Mindbenders* has been repeatedly extended—in fact, LucasFan's first project was an extension of that game titled *The New Adventures of Zak McKracken*. That game picked up where the first left off with its story of an alien-fighting tabloid writer (Fox). While the art is mostly pulled from and styled off of the original game, the project still showed its roots as an amateur effort: the puzzles and narrative were not yet fully developed. A range of other independent projects exist, some complete and some not, that have similar ambitions of extending the story. The *King's Quest* series also has a wealth of small projects surrounding it. Among them is *King's Quest 2.5*, a game intended to fill the gap in time between the second and third games in the series. That project followed the same style as the original games.

Fanfiction brings with it an attitude toward the text as ever-evolving, as Bronwen Thomas describes: "Individual stories, and even the source texts themselves, are conceived as being subject to constant modification and expansion. Authors, however much they might be revered, are conceived of as participants in an ongoing conversation, their creativity and handling of narrative technique seen as something to be engaged with rather than admired from afar" (217). This conversational metaphor recalls Ryan's definition of interactivity as dialogue, extending interactivity beyond any one individual work and opening the door to viewing fanfiction (and fan games) as in continual dialogue with the "original" text, expanding and rewriting its boundaries. This interactivity also recalls the importance of the ractor to Nell's experiences with the Primer. The text enables interaction as much as it is a site of interaction, and the social experience of a text (which the networked platform makes visible) is primary. No fan game is created in a vacuum: communal interaction is essential. This circumstance begins to demonstrate how fans interact with the genre itself, building on previous works (when permitted or ignored by copyright holders) to explore new frontiers.

CHAPTER 6

Personal Adventures

Thalia James, member of the Earth Anti-Encroachment League for over twenty years, has contracted a bizarre disorder during an inspection of a distant planet. Now it seems that danger is always two steps behind her as she continues what she once considered a relatively mundane job. It seems as if there is something rotten in the state of the Milky Way. . . .

That was the summarizing paragraph for the adventure game I was going to star in . . . before it got cancelled.

However, for a game character, being cancelled is hardly the end of the world. In fact, there's an entire universe beyond the one that you Outsiders see on your screens whenever you start playing our games . . . and for the first time, you're going to get a look at it. (Akril15, "Adventure: The Inside Job" [2008])

WHILE REMAKES are essential to fan communities (particularly as they preserve and enhance playability of foundational stories), the community of *Adventure Game Studio* and other creators has also given rise to a range of original works—including some that have in turn inspired their own fan engagement. It is impossible to do justice here to the entire range of games produced: the *AGS* website alone lists over a thousand titles ranging from the completely unplayable to one-room puzzle games to full-length and award-winning adventure games. Many of these games are identified with a solo author, although the use of communal resources and shared materials is common practice. It is tempting to label these games as independent games; however, that label has been co-opted by major marketplaces such as Xbox Live's Indie Game section and is a commercial designation that serves a purpose akin to the designation of "indie" film. While the "indie" label denotes a process of production by small teams working with fewer resources than the producers of mainstream game titles, the label is often used as a short-hand for "quirky" or "retro." The typically noncommercial ambitions of most fan games and *AGS* adventure games deserve their own categorization, though here existing terminology falls short. Certainly, such games fall under the rubric of playable media (Wardrip-Fruin), but that category is also far broader. Thus I prefer the label "personal games," referring both to the scale of the projects and the tendency toward personal storytelling that an accessible medium with a shallow learning curve for creation and a free distribution platform enables. Anna Anthropy associated individual authorship with the ability to express an idea through production and create "more personal games, more relevant games, more games with something to say." Adventure games, with their focus on experiential personal narratives, are an ideal form within the personal games movement. Within this genre, stories range from an artist struggling to overcome a cold and win the attention of a gallery (*A Cure for the Common Cold*, by MashPotato, *AGS* 2007) to the story of a wounded solider trying to recover his memory (*Purgatorio*, by Johanas, *AGS* 2007). Games within the *AGS* archive are categorized by setting, genre, and story type, revealing a range of combinations that I begin to explore through some exemplars of the form.

FAN GAME AS EDITORIAL

Personal games can include fan works, ranging from the sequels and remakes I've already examined to works that further diverge and use the platform as a space for reflecting on and parodying the adventure game genre. A project that diverges more than is common from the genre's roots was announced in 2001 and then summarily canceled by the team responsible for the *King's Quest* remakes. Titled *Royal Quest* (2001, *AGS*), this project was intended as a parody of the series. The team released a few screenshots revealing its intentions, and a preview described the vulgar South Park–style humor of the parody, subtitled "Retrieving Lost Shit" (Wells). The team abandoned the project with the explanation that it intended to restore the standing of classic games and did not want to undermine its own efforts by releasing such a mean-spirited-seeming parody. The game essentially disappeared from even Internet gossip—except, in the spirit of the fan remake, by the occasional person who claims that he or she will eventually produce his or her own version of the abandoned project. The same Internet communities that distribute the more faithful remakes keep this rumor alive, and perhaps it is from their midst that a new fan or a fan coauthor will emerge to follow through.

The adventure game community talks about some projects more than others—especially games that received accolades or positive responses on multiple websites or that were given various awards. Fans recognize some projects that reflect community values, such as: *Adventure: The Inside Job* (2008; hereafter *ATIJ*) was built as a swan song for the classic era, and thus appeals strongly to other player-creators. *ATIJ* drew its material from both finished and unfinished games, inviting the player to take the role of a character from an unreleased game running through scenes from a number of classic and obscure titles. The story opens doors that appeared in the original games but could never be opened, entering spaces that were nothing more than set-dressing in the original, and thus literally exploring beyond the edges of the designer's world. In plate 7, the contrast of styles, scale, and pixelation in sprites pulled from different video games into one shared setting is clear. This combination of originality and the complete remix of both familiar and unfamiliar elements pushes the game beyond expectations of "fan" production and toward "original" work, if such a dichotomy can even be sustained. The game's creator, Akril, noted that "in some ways, *ATIJ* can be considered a fangame, which would make it one the few fangames that includes ripped graphics and music yet isn't a sequel, a remake or a spinoff" (Akril15, "Adventure: The Inside Job" [2008]). In this, Akril has hit on the very qualities that distinguish the work even from parodies like the abandoned *Royal Quest*.

This different status—a fan work that is not a spinoff but instead a metafiction for the adventure game genre—allows the game to exist as a critique of corporate production. Through its very premise, it draws its material from truly abandoned games, the type of games most of whose content exists only within the inaccessible confines of the corporate vault. The game is not only a tribute but a satire, a reminder of the potential lost with each abandoned idea that is allowed to languish, incomplete. It is reminiscent of Flourish Klink's interactive fiction *Muggle Studies*, which, as previously discussed, editorializes on the very construction of *Harry Potter*.

Akril's stated intention was "to appeal to people who not only love adventure games, but have played too freaking many adventure games" (Akril15, "Adventure: The Inside Job" [2008]). This wording is interesting: the game's creator suggests that appreciation of a game like this, with its critique of the death of the genre, is only possible for those who have been immersed in the adventure game canon. Given the demise of many adventure games on the corporate cutting room floor as the golden age came to an end, Akril's work also serves as a poignant reminder of the games that could have been as well as those that were made and loved—and the shift in power from interactive fiction produced under the auspices of corporate production teams to the freedom to recombine and reimagine granted to the fan turned creator. As the main character, Thalia, the player is trying to save adventure games from "genrecide" while going through a series of familiar games tracking a villain, often passing through doors that were blocked in the original games. Akril acknowledges that the story structure, with characters from canceled games able to move between game worlds to keep the genre alive, is inspired by Jasper Fforde's *Thursday Next* series with travel between literary worlds (Akril). While characters and settings from classic games—including *Space Quest, Indiana Jones and the Fate of Atlantis*, and *Leisure Suit Larry*—appear out of place in the same space, they are appropriately juxtaposed by a shared purpose in narrative, and given a life beyond their home gamespace by Akril's work. Several of the rooms in the game are real but unreachable rooms Akril uncovered from viewing the resource files of released games from LucasArts and Sierra (Akril). Even the mix of visual styles clearly evident in any screenshot from the game (including plate 7) evokes the diversity of the genre while also serving as a nostalgic homage to past creators—as with Club Scumy, named in reference to the LucasArts gaming engine.

The game's success as an in-joke heavy adventure game with its own metafiction and Akril's own interest in continuing the story of these forgotten characters spurred a sequel, *Adventure: All in the Game*. The two games would be difficult to parse for a newcomer to the genre, as much of the humor and gameplay depends upon recognizing the ways the creator is inspired by and builds upon elements from earlier classic games. This buildup of interactions shows the movement of an author and a community from playing, to responding to those same games, to creating new works. Such developments are a defining aspect of fandom, as the shared story of the genre's history is as important to this community's adventure games as any particular narrative from one of the many series that has been represented and extended.

Fan adventure games such as Akril's take an editorial stance highly informed by the idea of the player as both audience and creator, and what Ian Bogost would call the "procedural rhetoric" of Akril's world reflects the adventure game genre back upon itself. Bogost defines "procedural rhetoric" as making an argument through simulation and rule-based systems rather than through writing or images (14). This is the kind of argument that games make. However, he cautions against understanding a system's coded argument (its designer's intention) as free of player influence, because player agency in games of all kinds leads to unique interpretations of play experiences. In games and other rules-based systems, meaning generation is created by the players, who set the work's processes into motion (Bogost 17). Few outside of the adventure game–making communities would even recognize the ghosts of games within Akril's games, but in walking the line between recycled and original content, the creator draws attention to the convergence of both "folk art" genre work and interactive literary aspirations within the player-creator community. The term "player-creator" is as full of false binary inflection as is "reader-player"—nearly all creators of games must be players of games in some fashion, and the reader-player is always creating his or her experience.

Original games with intertextual fan legacies point toward the same gradual evolution and repurposing of story that any storytelling medium experiences. Just as some audiences continue to find satisfaction in revisiting the adventures of Sherlock Holmes and rewriting them for everything from steampunk to modern settings, the reoccurrence of patterns is well documented in games. Just as those texts cannot be fully grasped without reference to the original, so too are the works of player-creators woven with the threads of adventure games past from commercial, fan, and original storytellers. Some, like *ATIJ* and its sequel, wear those connections on their sleeve. Others are more clearly divorced from their predecessors, but no less important for understanding the tapestry of evolving interactive storytelling that such communities have helped to spin.

Whereas many of these games, including Akril's, adopted the aesthetics of the golden age adventure games along with their characters and narrative threads, other fan developers sought to push their favorite stories toward the future they might have had given advancements throughout the industry. However, the obvious financial limitations of a fan collective would seem to prevent it from building a modern computer game: production costs have grown alongside the rising numbers of dedicated 3-D modelers, engine programmers, and other specialists dedicated to any major game production today. And of course, all of the fan projects discussed thus far have been completed without hope of profit, as the intellectual property and copyright laws still favor coporate creators. While some creators might welcome fan productions and allow them to be distributed freely, the inability of fans to sell their works bars them from entrance into the commercial marketplace.

SAMPLE GAMES

I have already examined several personal games that clearly transform or depend upon other texts from the adventure game genre. However, personal adventure games are often in dialogue with both one another and the classics of the genre, relying on intertextuality. Intertextuality is at its most basic the notion of the path that connects meaning to previous texts. These connections do not need to be the conscious intention of the author; indeed, in the world of literary criticism, critics identify such connections among different works while paying little attention to the author's intent. One example of a strongly intertextual comic adventure game, *Out of Order*, was released by Hungry Software in 2000. It is not an *AGS* production: it is built with a system called *SLUDGE* that the creator designed entirely to meet the needs of his game. The artistic style of the game is not particularly evolved from the traditional style of the genre. The cartoon graphics, as shown in plate 8, are at a slightly higher resolution than in the early games. The style adds to the whimsical atmosphere throughout the journey of Hurford Schlitzing, the protagonist. That journey is both surreal and ordinary at the same time—there are echoes of familiar cartoon worlds. In a typical encounter in *Out of Order*, the player faces an alien doctor (shown in plate 8). Hurford observes the alien with suspicion: "He looks . . . slimy. Wouldn't want him prodding around in my intestines." The situation's humor is amplified by Hurford's own appearance, still dressed in a bathrobe and slippers. As he tries to outsmart the alien doctor into treating him for nonexistent symptoms, he attempts to swipe a bumper sticker and is chastened. Hurford replies: "So much for the red-equals-communism theory."

Like Akril's games, *Out of Order* draws upon a range of sources for intertextual references. *Out of Order*'s main character, Hurford Schlitzing, "stuck in this strange environment with only his pajamas and teddy-bear slippers," resembles the hapless Arthur Dent from Douglas Adams's *The Hitchhiker's Guide to the Galaxy*, a novel I discussed earlier as interactive fiction (LaVigne). Spotting the connection to the classics gives fans great enjoyment. This kind of referencing has most recently been popularized by the postmodern cartoon show *Family Guy* (1999–, television). Viewers are presented with coded symbols that draw on television shows, films, and other media. Interpreting the episodes fully requires knowledge well beyond the closed text of a single episode or even of the series as a whole. To merely quantify *Family Guy*'s influences, such as *The Simpsons* (1989–, television) and various family sitcoms, does not begin to reveal the symbols at work in the text. The process of decoding can be attempted without awareness of the works being referenced, but such an interpretation is incomplete: in the semiotic model of interpretation, knowledge of the cultural encyclopedia and related texts is essential to decoding meaning. This idea destroys the notion that writers are creating something new; instead, the writer's only power is textual collage, the ability to create "a multidimensional space in which a variety of writings, none of them original, blend and clash" (Barthes 146). The idea of "clashing" evokes the remix and the cacophony of voices and illustrative styles at work in a patchwork piece such as *ATIJ*. The *Family Guy*'s writers are, as Barthes puts it, orchestrators of the "already-written." The viewer is invited to participate in this self-conscious form of intertextuality as being "in" on the joke creates part of the essential pleasure of viewing. Similarly, the intertextuality of *Out of Order* is intentional and implies its own audience that is willfully held separate from a traditional commercial audience. This game's ideal player must have an understanding of science fiction, membership in the fan game community, and a relationship with more traditional literary texts—the text implies its own reader.

Even more grounded in referential narrative is a 2004 game entitled *Cirque de Zale* (*AGS*), a game created by Rebecca Clements, who is also notable as one of the few known female creators working within the realm of personal games. *Cirque de Zale's* graphics are closer to the classic games of early LucasArts, with a low resolution and simple color palette. The game, shown in plate 9, centers on a boy named Zale sent through a portal to a fantasy world whose residents suppose him to be the answer to all of their prayers—in particular, they believe he has come to rescue an imprisoned princess. The expectations set by the genre are very clear: in the classics like the *King's Quest* and *Quest for Glory* (1989–1998, various platforms) series, the boy would promptly assume his destined role as hero. Instead, in this parody Zale dedicates himself to starting a circus, noting that rescuing the princess sounds dangerous and generally like a bad idea. When at one point he is kidnapped by the same person who captured the princess because of that expectation that he'd fulfill the hero's role, as shown in plate 9, he walks right past the trapped princess and leaves her to her fate: he doesn't have the key, and he can't free her even if he wanted to. The player can try any approach possible, but the game will not let the player rescue the princess. She's left to rot in the cell, in complete contradiction of the classic era assumptions about the role of a hero. The designer described her intention to evoke the tradition of LucasArts adventures: "I wanted people to get a real sense of nostalgia as they played it, which is exactly the kind of game I'd love to play" (Manos).

The creator's statement here does not mean that her game is a reproduction of the classic genre. Aside from its aesthetics and narrative style,

Cirque de Zale plays with many of the standards of the genre, and Zale's antics little resemble that of the traditional game heroes who always accepted their quests. The game rejects the commercial formula even as it claims to be a descendent of the classics. It is evoking nostalgia, perhaps, but that nostalgia is colored with a realization that the players have grown up and their expectations have changed. The story is like a postmodern retelling of a folktale that rejects the paths and values of the original tale even as it pays homage to it in the act of reinterpretation. It also acts as wish-fulfillment for every player who has wished to deviate from the proscribed script of a quest story, for while it too follows its own narrative arc, it does so by deliberately rejecting what would once have been an assured and well-trodden path.

Another *Adventure Game Studio* release, *A Tale of Two Kingdoms* (2007, *AGS*), shows more concern with graphics and convincing atmosphere—the same elements typical of commercial innovation. *A Tale of Two Kingdoms* wears some of its intertextuality on its sleeve, from its Dickensian name to its many fairy-tale elements. Created by a Dutch team of experienced designers, the game includes wandering nonplayer characters and allows for multiple endings, an element that remains challenging for any game to incorporate convincingly. Part of what makes the atmosphere convincing is that the team has created a world for nonlinear play: this is particularly difficult when presenting a fairy-tale world, which is familiar territory for most gamers. One way they achieve this goal is by imagining nonplayer characters as people going about their everyday lives, a feature that one reviewer commented upon as unusual in this type of game:

> I was particularly charmed by the town, where you see many game characters and "extras" strolling around, going about their business as you might expect in a real town. This is a marked contrast to so many games that are full of abandoned villages, characters who just hang around in one spot waiting for you to come and talk to them, and huge metropolises that never actually seem to have anyone in them. (MacCormack)

The games to which the reviewer is referring could easily be those typical of the classic era, the personal games community today, or even modern commercial games—the stationary nonplayer character is a model established by the limitations of classic systems that has now become a familiar feature. *A Tale of Two Kingdoms* has the feel of what Sierra might produce today had it not abandoned the genre: it is not a fan game in the way that a direct *King's Quest* sequel would be, but it is highly informed by those classics in design and play. Such a game appears to be the truest form of homage, resembling the canon much more than *Cirque de Zale*, but even it displays a trajectory of innovation. The creators are not merely reproducing that which commercial creation once built; they are expanding upon the genre and in the process even redefining the mold.

Perhaps the most innovative individual game in recent years is an experimental game entitled *What Linus Bruckman Sees When His Eyes Are Closed* (2006). Creator Vince Twelve's adventure game is designed around two stories occurring at once. The designer explains the concept: "If someone could read my mental design document they would have read about two worlds, completely unconnected except by gameplay, as different as possible in mood, art, sound, and writing. One, a sad film evocative of a Kurosawa classic except rooted in Japanese mythology, the other an upbeat Saturday morning cartoon about an alien working at an interstellar burger joint. The player would play the two games simultaneously" (Twelve). Gameplay in *Linus Bruckman* is true to this vision of connected narratives. The difference in styles between the two linked games is staggering: the highly cartoonish imagery of the one contrasts with the surreal mysticism of the other, as shown in plate 10. The *AGS* community gave *Linus Bruckman* their award for innovation, acknowledging the move in a direction very different from the classic-era games while keeping many of the hallmarks of the genre's playable avatar and puzzles. If the top and bottom narrative were separated into distinct games, each would more resemble a classic adventure game in content. However, those two games would be incomplete, as much of the experience is embedded in finding and exploiting the connections between the two narratives.

A game like *Linus Bruckman* is no longer concerned about a dialogue with commercial works. Like several entries in the "Mystery House Taken Over" project, it is pushing the limits of the form as art. Such a game is as well suited for discussion by the critics of electronic literature as it is for informed feedback from the *AGS* community; it might even be in the former realm that it finds its closest aesthetic compatriots. I return to Lessig's thoughts on communities of remixers, whose "showing is valuable, even when the stuff produced is not" (Lessig, *Remix* 77). *Linus Bruckman* is valuable, both in its showing and in its innovations. It transcends the expectations of the amateur creator and the limitations of *Adventure Game Studio* (rightly winning the community's award for innovation in scripting), reminding its audience that traditional production has its own limits that a creator in this medium can defy. This game does not resemble any game of the classic era of adventure games—it redefines the linearity and progression of the form in a way that fragments and unifies its player's attention.

Games like *Linus Bruckman* coexist in the "announced games" list of *Adventure Game Studio* right alongside deliberately derivative fan games. While particularly exceptional fan games or remakes gain recognition on their own merits, others, such as the *Maniac Mansion Episodes* (2005–2008, *AGS*) by Rayman, Rocco, and several other creators, are more clearly tied to the original work. The *Maniac Mansion Episodes* are an extended series of short games in which the characters from the original LucasArts game participate in various further mysteries—the mystery house is never closed. These games are not particularly inventive in story, as the puzzles are along the lines of finding the key to allow two of the characters to escape the cellar, but they reflect the original series in style and in humor. Another example, AgentBauer's *Space Quest IV.5* (2008, *AGS*), accomplishes a familiar task of fan games by filling in the missing interlude between *Space Quest IV* and its official sequel. Similarly, the *Indiana Jones* franchise, which LucasArts developed during the classic era, is the starting point of Rob Shattock's *Indiana Jones—Coming of Age* (2008, *AGS*). The narrative Shattock chose to extend is not from the adventure games; instead, the story takes its cue from the films.

Other fan games are narratives that rework characters and settings, both classic and modern, with a variety that can be seen in examining any year of released *AGS* projects. Ghost's *Once Upon a Crime* (2008, *AGS*) is not a fan game derived from a previous adventure game, but like the pop culture phenomenon *Shrek*, it does reinterpret familiar fairytale archetypes. Similarly, Elen Heart's *Once Upon a Time* (2008, *AGS*) is a traditional fairy tale presenting mostly well-known characters and settings. Marion's *James in Neverland* (2008, *AGS*) offers beautiful environments to portray a Neverland inspired by James M. Barrie's *Peter Pan*. Another fan game from the same creator, *Dread Mac Farlane 2* (2008, *AGS*), is an adaptation of a French comic book of the same name—and also the sequel to a game Marion created earlier. Both games incorporate original elements, but the primary focus of Marion's work is reinterpreting narratives. Other fan games adhere more closely to the narratives in their source material. Ultra Magnus's work is inspired graphically and to some extent narratively by television. His game, *The New Kids*, uses the Icelandic television show *Lazytown* as a framework. (Games like this are a sign of the international membership of the *AGS* community. Even though it has few members, they come from all over the world. Indeed, *AGS* has released games in French, Italian, and German, and cooperation among *AGS* members allows for frequent translations of fan games for players who don't know the creator's language.) Skerrigan's *Doctor Who—Episode 0* (2008, *AGS*) draws upon the familiar world of the television and radio program for a two-room game, the narrative of which could translate easily into the *Doctor Who* canon.

REALITY-ON-THE-NORM

Another *AGS* phenomenon is an interlinked series of games tied not to any external world but instead to a continuing world generated by the community. This collective action perhaps transcends the label of personal games, as it demonstrates play that moves beyond individual games and authorship to generate a communal experience for players and creators to traverse at will. These games are referred to as the Reality-on-the-Norm, or RON, games. Members of the RON project describe the collective as involving "the creation of a central environment—in our case, the Reality-on-the-Norm town. Each member of the team creates his or her own game as a chapter to be added to all the previously achieved ones, thus creating a collective and diverse 'book' of several independent yet coherent chapters" (Reality-on-the-Norm). The first episode, "Lunchtime of the Damned," was released by Ben Croshaw in

2001. Shown in plate 11, the game showcases some of the characters and town settings ubiquitous in the series along with its surreal elements: the first involves resurrecting zombies. The project is a microcosm of the type of collaboration and overlapping narrative that is a strength of *AGS* as a creative community, with the strongest interactivity not in a single game but in the whole experience. Participating in the RON games as a creator requires abiding by the collective's rules. For instance, authors are not allowed to kill any of the characters within the town, nor are they allowed to claim the work of others as their own. The collective provides backgrounds and characters as well as a persistent narrative that is continually expanding. RON games can vary greatly in content and audience, as the distance between Brentimous's *Rock—A True Story* (2008 *AGS*), a game about a young would-be rock star on a quest to save music, and Bitby's mature audience RON game, *Au Naturel* (2008 *AGS*), a game about a man on a quest for nude photos, demonstrates.

The RON community has even generated its own fan community. Its home page features fanfiction and fan art, some of which juxtapose the RON characters with classic genre icons. The central hubs of the RON community include work by both the "original" creators of the concept and fans who have joined the efforts later. The shared universe resembles commercial worlds like Marvel's or DC's comic universes or TSR's (now Wizards of the Coast and Hasbro's) *Dragonlance*, but those series impose barriers on their expansion. Not just anyone can extend the universe: the would-be creator's efforts have to be approved by the intellectual property holders, and only authorized projects become part of the canon of the commercial universe. RON demonstrates how such a universe can exist and thrive on a communal model of authorship and responsibility, determined by participants rather than imposed by an authority.

The *AGS* games demonstrate a constant focus on innovation of all kinds, signaling that this community is not stagnant but a dynamic group from which new canon-worthy works might form entirely outside the purview of commercial media. Among the many innovative games, a few stand out for offering original elements, particularly in terms of artistry. Creamy's *Bob Escapes* (2008, *AGS*) offers art unusual within the digital medium, as the settings appear to have been drawn by hand using colored pencils, while Eugene Couto's *The Oracle* (2006, *AGS*) heads the opposite direction with backgrounds taken from photos shot on location. *Nanobots* (2008, *AGS*), a collaboration between The Ivy and Vince Twelve (of *Linus Bruckman* fame), is a particularly high-quality game created by two people who might be considered among the stars of the *AGS* community. The narrative of *Nanobots* pits tiny self-aware robots against an evil professor and thus plays with perspective and philosophies of artificial intelligence. Ivan Dixon's *Sydney Treads the Catwalk* (2008, *AGS*), which focuses on the life of a homeless man thrust into the spotlight, is the work of a professional comics artist adapting his own work to a new medium.

While the audiences for the games released vary greatly—some creators admit that their works are intended originally for their own family or friends, while others aspire to draw in fans of particular genres or of other narratives—none goes entirely ignored on the *AGS* forum. The proportion of fan games to original creations suggests a greater interest in original narratives, even if those narratives themselves often acknowledge their debt to other sources. Comparing the imagery of these games reveals great variation in approaches, as the absence of editorial control means that games of any genre, style, or quality can be brought to the attention of the community. Games that fit or extend the adventure game genre are most likely to fit the community's values, but unusual games that rework the engine to accommodate unexpected mechanics and genres are also released and noted. The community rewards good work with attention, and games that are bug-ridden or show insufficient craft are quickly forgotten. Games that attract an audience continually rise to the top of the forums and are kept alive in the archives of the community game list to form, perhaps, a sampling of the classics of narrative games.

ADVENTURE GAME STUDIO AND LITTLE BIG PLANET

Adventure Game Studio is not the only tool that enables people to create games. One of the more interesting commercial tools with a communal release structure is *Little Big Planet* (2008, Playstation 3), a game and toolset that provides an internal set of worlds where players can build and share their own levels and even narrative experiences. In this type of community, the direct corporate sponsorship influences what can be created. The creators of such corporately produced tools usually design them with clear limitations, although occasionally content-creators can exceed those. The original game holds several worlds with platformer gameplay focused on guiding the smiling and customizable "Sackboy" avatar through challenges involving jumping, timing, and other reflex-based actions. The levels included in the purchased game (enough to "fill" a world) provide some gameplay, but the game is constantly extended by users who populate additional worlds with their own levels. Each user-created world is its own level, often with its own internal narrative. Players are limited to the resources of the platformer toolkit, which comes with prebuilt objects that players can position and modify to build their level. Some of the resulting levels offer narrative and gameplay that the original game designers never intended. Take, for instance, two different simulations of 9/11 built within *Little Big Planet*. These levels both position the player as an attacker, using the friendly "Sackboy" and quirky world pieces to re-create destruction. The pushing of boundaries of the platformer in these examples seems to be more about what a builder can get away with than what he or she can create.

Environments like *Little Big Planet* encourage intertextual creativity within a community of shared levels, but the ends are very different than those of a communal creation space like *Adventure Game Studio* affords. The *AGS* community chooses their influences and the extent to which commercial creations impact their work—in *Little Big Planet*, the corporate creators determine what objects are available and design the world builder tools. *AGS* allows creators to import their own assets and thus control the entire artistic feel of the world, while *Little Big Planet* restricts players to an official set of building blocks and 3-D parts. Another contrast is there is no guarantee that *Little Big Planet* content, once created by a player, will remain available within the gamespace. The corporate owners have the ability to remove content they consider offensive and to censor what appears, producing a dialogue between commercial and communal in which the commercial world always seems to have the final say. *AGS* relies on community designations for mature content and describes its forums as "pretty much a free-for-all" (Snarky).

Even if a game were banned from the forums and site, the author could still distribute it elsewhere: the creator of a level in *Little Big Planet* cannot remove it from that ecosystem.

The play of power within *Little Big Planet* expresses, at least for the moment, a symbiotic relationship between the shared and commercial economy. In this case, money flows only to the corporate owner of the space as players pay for the game and, with it, access to the creation tools and user-created levels, and player-creators are only rewarded by earning good reputations. However, the commercial incentives for corporations to provide spaces for creation are clear: user-generated content extends the length of the game and offers different play experiences to engage players, without the corporate investment of paying for more level design. This model only works for creators as long as the process of creation is "fun" enough to keep them from feeling like cogs in a production system. The same warning that Lessig applied to remix culture in the hybrid economy holds for traditional modders and level producers in Sony's *Little Big Planet* game platform: unless they are being rewarded monetarily, the act of production must still hold the same ability to produce passion that an act outside of this commercial software might. Once money is involved, as it is in the world of *Second Life*, the tone of the production changes. Intellectual property ownership becomes important, and bickering between creators turns into legal disputes, such as a 2008 case brought in Florida by Kevin Alderman against another user who copied his virtual "interactive sex bed" code (Kirby). In such circumstances, commercial entanglement overwhelms the sharing economy, while by contrast, in spaces like *Little Big Planet* money flows only to the parent company, and player-creators are never rewarded beyond reputation.

We are currently negotiating the terms of Lessig's hybrid economy at a time when content is increasingly expected to be free. Paid production of content is dying in several traditional media as magazines and newspapers are taking new directions and exploring the possibilities of convergent media. In March 2010, *Variety* surprised its readers by abruptly firing the last of its full-time film reviewers, Todd McCarthy, in favor of relying solely on freelance work (Fritz). The decision has generated criticism, particularly in light of McCarthy's own perceived ability to attract readers as a highly experienced reviewer, but the transformation in the way people read movie reviews is working against him. The existence of highly popular content conglomeration sites such as Rotten Tomatoes makes it harder for any one critic's voice to be essential reading. Rotten Tomatoes takes a quick survey of reviews and uses them to give each film a score. Todd McCarthy has been one of their "top critics" since the beginning of the site, yet when he vanishes, his will be but one voice lost from the clamor of the crowd, and more voices will always emerge to fill any gaps. Freelance reviewers can be paid very little and offered few benefits as compared to staff reviewers. And some of the reviewers Rotten Tomatoes aggregates are completely unpaid but publish regularly enough to be worthy of the site.

Variety explained its decision to eliminate McCarthy's position as "being flexible in the face of economic realities" (Fritz). In an economy where the decision to cut content production by staff members can be justified, the opposite choice—to surrender the corporate stranglehold on intellectual property—seems the less likely path. Yet that is exactly the type of experiment with content that is emerging now, as the hybrid economy encourages U.S. companies to try to expand the influence of their ideas. None of these efforts yet resembles the freedom of production represented by *doujinshi* in Japan. Copyright lawyers in this country would have many reasons to object to moving toward such an open production system, and unlike Japan, this nation does not suffer from a lack of lawyers ready to prosecute perceived intellectual property threats.

Nevertheless, some experiments with the ceding of intellectual property restrictions, though not as open as the *doujinshi* model, suggest the possibility of cooperation between corporations and autonomous creators in the hybrid economy. One such project is BBC's Creative Archive project, an archive of materials from BBC broadcasts licensed under a variant of the Creative Commons standard for use in remixes, adapted to the needs of the U.K. system, where copyright law is well enforced. The license is hardly all-inclusive, and commercial concerns are still at the forefront of the BBC's concerns:

> The Creative Archive project has not been without critics from the commercial sector, worried that the BBC giving away their content for free

would make it difficult for them to be able to make money from their
own content. The BBC has explained to some of the commercial players
that the content would be limited during the pilot, would not be available in broadcast quality, and that watermarking technologies would be
trialled so that content could be recognised when it crops up elsewhere.
(WikiNews)

Despite these sorts of restrictions, the BBC archive is a step toward
legitimizing the cultural activities that would happen with or without
this program. By creating a virtual repository of content formatted for
remixing, however, the BBC can actually enhance the power of its own
imagery. The BBC archives seek to expand awareness of the company's
content and perhaps even to discover a few inspired creators who can
remix its work in ways that will connect with a modern audience. It is
in effect encouraging its own ideas to go viral by making it easier for a
commentator or fan to use images from BBC programs than from other
sources.

Releasing material from aired programs is one step. The U.K.'s Free
Culture group has suggested that the BBC go a step further and make
available material that has not been not aired, noting that

> such material, at least for the purposes of reuse, will likely be as valuable
> if not more valuable than that taken from complete programmes. As such
> the BBC should prioritise it for release equally with material taken from
> finished works. Given that the rights situation is likely to be simpler for
> such "non-programme material" it might even be sensible to focus on
> releasing this category of work rather than excerpts from publicly released
> programmes. (Cowlishaw et al. 2006)

Such material can include deleted scenes, outtakes, rehearsals, and other pieces of film that would otherwise be unavailable. Such a move on
the part of the game industry would address the problem, lamented by
the fan community, of unreleased abandoned games languishing in the
vaults of Blizzard and other publishers. It would resurrect abandonware
from the cultural graveyard that the fan-created game *Adventure: The
Inside Job* so pointedly mocks.

I have observed repeatedly that corporations engaged with the hybrid economy can gain value from their relationship with fan-producers, whether through increased recognition and long-term presence of their games or through cooperative content generation that expands innovation for an entire form. Bethesda Softworks, creators of the *Elder Scrolls* series, re-released its earliest installments as free downloads to celebrate the tenth anniversary of the series and to draw attention to the latest commercial release. Sierra went a step further when it released *Mystery House* to the public domain, making it freely available for remixing and modification. Revolution software released *Beneath a Steel Sky* and revealed the source code, and several of *Doom*-publisher id Software's game engines have been freely released. Can we expect every company to begin ceding its intellectual property rights and throwing its ideas into public space? Of course not. But each of these cases—Bethesda and the BBC—suggests a willingness to negotiate new boundaries. Copyright law cannot kill the remix: even if these companies wanted to, there are not enough lawyers in the world. This practice is not going away; rather, it is growing, and it can lead to innovation as it spirals and builds upon itself.

THE SILVER LINING

While many of the works highlighted thus far have relied upon tools such as *Adventure Game Studio* to re-create the technical affordances of early adventure game platforms, not all fan games have followed in this path. Another group of fans networking across the world decided to take on the ambitious project of creating a full sequel to the *King's Quest* games using modern 3-D graphics and technology. The project, now called *The Silver Lining* (2010–2012, PC), was almost shut down by legal entanglements and the problem of copyright. Like fanfiction and fan film projects, a fan-created game sequel like this one violates the original copyright holders' claim, but like those projects, such games often go unchallenged unless they reach a certain scale. As the team now explains on its website, originally the copyright holders asked them to shut down: "On September 30, 2005, the team was asked to cease production by Vivendi Universal Inc., the owners of the *King's Quest* franchise. After weeks of negotiations and with the support of our fans, on November 29, 2005, Vivendi granted the team permission to legally continue production on the game" (Phoenix Studios). The passion of the fans for the project—both those directly involved and those eagerly awaiting their chance to play the game—was the turning point, according to the producers, in allowing the game production to continue. Vivendi's full reasons are open to speculation; however, the public nature of the outcry (and the perception that the company was persecuting the most dedicated of fans with no real commercial stakes threatened) likely played a role. The only concession the fan author group had to make was removing the label of *King's Quest* from the project, so the game would not be confused with a legitimate creation of the original copyright holders and was instead clearly under a "fan license." However, the rights continued to change hands when Vivendi merged with Activision in 2008, and Activision demanded a removal of all references and project materials from the web. A community movement to "Save *The Silver Lining*" sprang up, and the Phoenix team discussed options, including trying to purchase the rights to *King's Quest* outright (Matos). Hope came in a press release in which Activision directly cited the pressure from fans in 2010: "Given the overwhelming community support for *The Silver Lining* project, Activision is in discussions with Phoenix Online Studios about allowing them to continue to finish the game and then release it to their fans" (Totilo). Shortly after, Phoenix released a new trailer announcing its return. The first episode was released in July 2010.

The Silver Lining stands out from the other fan adventure games in part because of the intense production values at work. Often games produced with imitations of classic engines rely upon limited production resources, retro graphics, and outdated technology—the simplicity of the interface and production process, which allows an individual or small team to accomplish a great deal, does not necessarily enable them to meet the expectations players bring to mainstream industry titles for graphics or seamlessness of gameplay. These independent creators or small teams are usually operating with only their own money, no hope of compensation, and only their free time to devote to the project—heightening the appeal of point-and-click design tools that limit the amount of knowledge such a creator needs to implement his or her design. Other *King's Quest* fan sequels adhere primarily to this more familiar personal game model, including works such as *King's Quest 2.5*, intended to fill small gaps within the series, or even the comparatively transformative efforts of the previously mentioned AGDI to rebuild the first games in the series to meet the aesthetic and narrative quality set by later installments. The dated feel of most such independent projects hearkens back to the days before gaming was taken over by corporations with large resources. The old-fashioned graphics and interfaces give the impression that this world lacks innovation; to an outsider, it can look entirely stagnant, with graphics and interfaces reflecting traditions of classic 2-D side-scrolling games. As I argued earlier, these games often innovate in other areas, such as story or presentation, but because of the circumstances of their creation, they are not at the forefront of major technical innovation. They offer a chance for a fan voice to tell a story in this medium, but that voice is rarely heard outside the underground game community.

But *The Silver Lining* does not suffer from these limits: the team behind it used high production graphics and technology, even though the game has the same humble origins as other independent efforts. Episode 1, as shown through a screenshot in plate 12, reimagines Sir Graham as an older man (still in his iconic blue hat) traveling outside the familiar land of Daventry into hostile 3-D islands. There was no corporate powerhouse behind *The Silver Lining* project, and no one on the creative team was being paid. The first four game installments have been released for free, whereas a comparable effort by a corporation could conceivably be priced at $30 to $40 a copy. The development team, which appropriately calls itself Phoenix Online Studios, explains the driving motivations:

> The first [aim] is to bring the genre of adventure gaming back to its roots while giving it an overhaul of new elements such as the contemporary graphic format and more attention given to plot rather than random "pixel hunting" . . . [and] to create a community for our fellow adventure gamers where they can be given what they miss from the golden days and

provide a space where they do not feel so isolated from the current trends of the gaming industry. (Silver Lining)

Phoenix Online Studios here acknowledges one of the primary motives of fan authors: the pleasure of other fans in the values that this particular style of game embodies. Furthermore, it notes the importance of plot, echoing the emphasis on story-driven adventures expressed by the original team behind the *King's Quest* series. This juxtaposition perhaps expresses the reason for revisiting this particular series, as opposed to one of the many other genre titles that have gone without new installments, while also revealing a desire for taking the best from "current trends" in the gaming industry as evident in the graphical emphasis.

This is not the end of the story for Phoenix Online. As of June 2013, four episodes of *The Silver Lining* were released, with the presumptive final episode five still pending. In keeping with the name the team chose, it seems to be rising again after several near flameouts from copyright shutdowns. The team has now released several episodes of their first commercial adventure game funded not by a typical corporate producer but by fans through crowd-sourcing. As is only appropriate for pioneers within the world of fan-produced interactive storytelling, they are now leading the way in developing funding models for adventure game projects that are also supporting the creation of games by the likes of Al Lowe (*Leisure Suit Larry*) and Tim Schafer (*Day of the Tentacle, Maniac Mansion*). This next step in rethinking the production process, particularly for this genre of narrative-driven games, suggests that fan involvement might be transforming all aspects of creation—including funding and distribution.

CHAPTER 7

Kickstarting a Genre

IN FEBRUARY 2012, the game studio Double Fine posted a Kickstarter campaign. The man behind the project? Company founder Tim Schafer, the creator of *Day of the Tentacle*, *Grim Fandango*, and many other classic games. Kickstarter uses preorders and incentives, along with social networking, to fund projects before they are available for sale. Several small game companies and aspiring designers turned to the platform for game fund-raising immediately, but none was a huge success until Tim Schafer launched his adventure game Kickstarter campaign. The campaign was started to fund "a small team under Tim Shafer's supervision [developing] . . . Double Fine's next game, a classic point-and-click adventure." The initial campaign post further offered fans a challenge: "for fans of adventure games, this is a chance to prove that there is still a large demand out there for a unique medium that inspired so many of us" (Schafer).

The campaign asked for $400,000 to fund the making of the game, and in return fans could get a variety of rewards, from a copy of the game once it was finished for a pledge of $15 to lunch with Tim Schafer and Ron Gilbert for $10,000. It was fully funded within eight hours of launch. Within twenty-four hours, the project had $1 million in pledges, higher than any Kickstarter project before it. But that number proved to be nothing next to the funding that would come. By the time the Kickstarter campaign came to an end, Tim Schafer's team raised over $3 million. Of Double Fine's backers, nearly 50,000 backers opted for what amounted to a preorder of the finished game (Schafer), while four backers bought lunch with Shafer and Gilbert. Every limited reward tier sold out, demonstrating that some fans were willing to spend a lot more than market value to see such a game come to fruition.

The rise of direct fan funding of adventure game projects has done much to prove the power of Kickstarter. News of the project immediately made its appearance on the *Adventure Game Studio* forums, with one fan noting, "Wow, this truly is amazing. Just on the promise of a new game, Double Fine raised enough capital *in a single day* to make it. I don't want to be presumptuous, but this is promising on a wider scope than just this one game. It could be the blossoming of a whole new way of funding video games, as this proves it can be a resounding success" (Scavenger). Of course, other fans noted that $400,000 was rather high for a point-and-click adventure, given what *Adventure Game Studio* creators could do without this type of major investment.

Double Fine's wildly successful campaign represented a giant leap forward from the proclaimed death of a genre, and clearly, fans answered the challenge of proving market demand for a form of storytelling that was once labeled as antiquated. The revitalization Double Fine's offer promised did not imply innovation in the form. Note the use of the word "classic" in the description, with the implicit contract to avoid action or other out-of-genre elements (Schafer). Instead, Double Fine promised a team working under a proven master storyteller. Beyond that, next to no details were offered or needed. The 87,142 backers were expressing their confidence in Tim Schafer, and in the thrill of having a "classic" adventure game once again. While some speculated or hoped that the game would be a sequel or extension of a remembered favorite, the backers ultimately gambled on a new and entirely unknown property (though similar Kickstarter projects have since used headliners such as *Leisure Suit Larry* to gather fans of a particular story to help stage that character's return to the digital stage). Many of these campaigns have been successful, if not nearly as over their funding targets as the Double Fine project: I will examine several campaigns, including Phoenix Online Studio's original adventure game and the *Leisure Suit Larry* reboot.

Double Fine's campaign is unusual in that Double Fine is a commercial studio, with a number of games already launched—this is not a collective of fully independent developers coming to crowdsourcing for funding. While a number of video games had already been funded with Kickstarter, these projects tended to be smaller both in funding and ambition. The platform had also been used primarily for the transition from independent game production to studio, with teams who'd proven their skills using their own shoestring budgets trying to raise the resources to fund larger games. Kickstarter was intended for projects more akin to the personal passion of *The Silver Lining* team, who did find their own supporters for an original adventure game through the same fund-raising method but did not achieve nearly the numbers of Tim Schafer's impressive haul. The co-opting of the platform by highly established designers pursuing more personal projects is also happening in other media genres, with successful campaigns recently held for a *Veronica Mars* film (based on a popular girl-detective TV show) and a new film from Zach Braff, known for the film *Garden State* and the television show *Scrubs*. Several of these projects have been met with a backlash as some argue that these creators could have funded their projects through normal sources and are using Kickstarter as a stunt and drawing attention away from real communal creativity.

What the Double Fine campaign makes clear, however, is that the adventure game is far from dead. What led to this stage of public resurrection from the death of the genre? And can the elements that helped bring adventure games back from commercially moribund to generously fan-funded be understood as part of the larger revitalization of interactive narrative and electronic literature? These Kickstarter successes are not isolated, but are part of a wider change in the industry centered on new platforms and models both for building and interacting with games—and story-centric games have benefited strongly from these new spaces.

Kickstarter is particularly powerful as a site for this type of creative development and reinvention: it has become synonymous with crowdsourced funding. Genres pronounced dead can be resurrected, experimental projects can be funded on the strength of a creator's résumé, and digital fund-raising can supplant the support of traditional investors. This revolution has been so influential in the games industry in particular that another company hoping to piggyback on Kickstarter's success launched a new site solely for crowd-sourcing game projects based in the Netherlands and offering a very different backer rewards system. The new site, "Gambitious," is rethinking the model of pledges in return for preorders and physical goods typical of Kickstarter campaigns, replacing it with one that mimics mainstream business investment, with potential players receiving dividends in proportion to their support and depending on the eventual success of a funded studio rather than just one particular title. This network of shared investment—and in a sense shared risk, as investors gamble that the resulting game and add-ins will be worth their upfront cash, or that other players will enjoy them enough to result in dividends—is not so far removed from the communal model of *Adventure Game Studio* and other creative networks or from the commercial model of the stock market, with the fan collective as one "Investor Cooperative" behind a game company. Rather than relying on venture capitalists or angel investors, it puts forward a highly communal model for development, with the same crowd as investors and as customers who will determine the product's eventual success. While the monetization is relatively new, the projects themselves reflect the same grassroots creative process.

In the introductory video to the Double Fine project, Tim Shafer explained the rationale for using Kickstarter. He noted that adventure games were his favorite type of game to make, but it seemed like even though "adventure games exist in our dreams and our memory," a publisher wouldn't fund the project. As a result, he decided that the game should be "a game for adventure fans, funded by adventure fans, and we want to make it with adventure fans" (Schafer). This focus on the fans not only as consumers but also as cocreators navigates what Matt Hills notes as the complex relationship between fan cultures and consumerism; he "considers fans to be simultaneously inside and outside processes of commodification, experiencing an intensely personal 'use-value' in relation to their object of fandom, and then being repositioned within more general and systemic processes of 'exchange-value'" (44). The economy of the Kickstarter project reflects the personal value fans find in this type of game—backers are invited into a community and given constant development reports and the opportunity to be heard throughout the process. This exchange hinges on the act of "donating," which is not without risk and is distanced from simply paying for a product. Kickstarter (and the company funded) offers no guarantee that any rewards will actually be received, and most rewards involve much more than simply preordering. The Double Fine tiers included options for signed posters, portraits of fans by game artists, and original art from the game. Funding of this kind works so well for drawing fan contributions in part because it is positioned not merely as preordering a game title but as participating in the process. Double Fine's promise that an entire community would have a voice and insight into the design process was a success.

TELLING TALES

While Kickstarter has been embraced as revolutionary, the reentry of the adventure game into commercial space began before the crowd-sourcing platform entered the picture. Hardware shifts, along with the expansion of the gaming market to more completely embrace casual game genres, led to several mainstream adventure game series both familiar and original returning to the marketplace—and often on plat-forms that were not so inclined toward point and click as the PC.

As you'll recall, the future of adventure game efforts was looking grim around the turn of the millennium. Big-name projects, such as a *Warcraft* graphic adventure game and an official LucasArts sequel to *Sam & Max Hit the Road*, were tabled. In 2004, after *Sam & Max 2* was canceled when it was rumored to be mostly finished, Randy Sluganski lamented in an article for one of the major adventure game fan sites on the web: "Adventure games are not, nor have they ever been, blockbuster products. They are what is known in the industry as 'evergreen' games because they sell month after month for years, steady but never spec-tacular yet in the long haul many of the games show impressive sales figures. But unfortunately, all that matters in today's marketplace are the sales figures for the first two months as retail space is at a premium and slow but steady is no longer welcome in the industry." However, (thanks to a well-negotiated contract that offers hope for the continuance of classic game titles) the rights to *Sam & Max* reverted back to the cre-ators a year after LucasArts abandoned the project, and the creators saw the potential to continue creating adventure games using the charac-ters with a smaller effort and online-only distribution. That project, *Sam & Max* by Telltale Games, won Imagine Game Network's (IGN) Best Adventure Game award for 2006: "Adventure gaming might still be on the critical list but *Sam & Max* is a good sign of its recovery" (IGN.com).

The studio those former LucasArts employees formed in 2004, Telltale Games, started with *Sam & Max* and quickly evolved into one of the most important adventure game publishers of the new age. The studio took advantage of digital distribution models in developing its innovative business model, releasing installments of games digitally for less than the price of a full game. This practice helped sustain the company with a steady revenue stream while it produced a series of smaller games and avoided the longer production cycles and major releases typical of the bigger studios. This model was already familiar to those who follow fan productions, as such games are often released in episodes or "chapters" to make up for the long periods of time amateur creators require to complete games on a part-time schedule. The release of installments recalls the serialized novels of print publishing, and, like them, the games often feature similar cliff-hangers and continuing stories.

The adventure games produced by Telltale Games hearken back to the original sensibility of adventure games by focusing on character development and story. The playable avatars of Sam and Max in particular remain icons for the adventure game community. As their creator, Steve Purcell, describes the pair, "Sam and Max are a pair of overzealous crime fighters. They call themselves Freelance Police because it gives them some unspecified license to do whatever they want. Sam is a six foot dog in a baggy gray suit and sharp fedora. Max is a three foot naked rabbity thing who sometimes packs a German Luger somewhere on his person. They roll through the streets in a smoking 1960 DeSoto Adventurer painted to look like a black and white squad car searching for wrongs to right, innocents to defend and jelly-filled sugar donuts to devour" (Linkola). The resurrection of unusual characters of this nature shows that mainstream game companies have returned at least for the moment to embracing the hallmarks of the adventure genre.

As Telltale Games has broadened its scope, it has resurrected other series and turned to other media for stories to adapt, including the *Bone* graphic novels, the *Fable* fairy-tale graphic novel adaptations, and even the *Back to the Future* films. While previously the studio had stuck to LucasArts titles, it acquired the rights to reboot the *King's Quest* series, a timely move given the interest AGDI remakes and *The Silver Lining* episodes have attracted. But despite this pending resurrection of the franchise, Telltale Games made no effort to distance *The Silver Lining* further from the series or halt the distribution of new episodes, keeping with its record of noninterference in fan productions. However, the company canceled the reboot as of April 2013.

One notable reboot courtesy of Telltale Games is *Tales of Monkey Island* (2009). Along with "special edition" remakes of the originals (*The Secret of Monkey Island: Special Edition* in 2009; *Monkey Island 2 Special Edition* in 2011), this installment-based sequel brought the classic franchise back to life nearly ten years after the last installment had failed to achieve much commercial success. Players were nervous about a repeat of recent failed sequels, and concerned to see a different company take over the LucasArts production. The designers responded to these concerns in the game's FAQ:

> WILL TALES OF MONKEY ISLAND BE EXACTLY LIKE I REMEMBER THE MONKEY ISLAND GAMES BEING WHEN I PLAYED THEM TEN YEARS AGO?
>
> Is this a trick question? We know fans have been imagining their own versions of a new Monkey Island game for a decade now, but we're not trying to make that sequel you dreamed up. . . . We're making something completely new. And Tales of Monkey Island will be just like you remember in the ways that really count. Funny characters? Check! Goofball humor? Check! Ridiculous storyline that lovingly spoofs pirate legend and lore? Check! (Telltale Games)

The key phrase "just like you remember in the ways that really count" shows the designer's courtship of the original fan base: older now, but still drawn to the familiar elements that shaped their first experience with these types of games. The rest of the response places the elements of narrative at the forefront, promising the same experience of character and storyline and saying nothing about the puzzles or gameplay itself. That omission suggests that the gameplay aspect is being allowed to evolve, to change, without betraying the core of the series. The designers are not simply imitating, making their own version of the David statue, but are expanding beyond the older mold. The fans that this FAQ addresses are those who "have been imagining their own versions of a new *Monkey Island* game for a decade now," but this description might be selling those fans short. Some had been imagining new fan games like this for over two decades—and many of them have done more than just imagine and have had more than a fling with the act of creation.

Aside from the remake of *The Secret of Monkey Island*, which resembles a fan update akin to the Sierra remakes, some of the classic producers have re-released their games. The first *Gabriel Knight* game, a supernatural murder detective franchise set in New Orleans, was just brought out in a digital-rights-management-free form for online download, and at $10 a download, it is clear that creators still think there is value in these older games (Jensen and Williams). The re-release of the *Gabriel Knight* game without digital-rights management shows a lessening of control, and an investment in the hybrid economy: this is particularly interesting given that designer Jane Jensen is also among those now using Kickstarter to support new projects. Such releases are not of interest to a large number of users, but they benefit from the "long tail" of the digital—they require no shelf space, need no inventory, and can be directly downloaded by the audience that would seek them out (Lessig, *Remix* 129). This kind of release is part of the reason why abandonware as such is hard to identify and the work of fan archivists faces the same consumer-producer conflict as the larger communities of transformative works. When a game can still return, decades later, and have a commercial audience, the old idea still has value, particularly as the source of remakes, sequels, and other transformations:

> Walk the streets of Florence and you'll find a copy of the David on practically every corner. For centuries, the way to become a Florentine sculptor has been to copy Michelangelo, to learn from the master. Not just the great Florentine sculptors, either—great or terrible, they all start with the master; it can be the start of a lifelong passion, or a mere fling. The copy can be art, or it can be crap. (Doctorow 89)

As in Cory Doctorow's observations of the city of Florence littered with David statues, in the world of games creators constantly revisit the original idea by one means or another. Roberta Williams appears to have been correct when she declared the adventure game genre still very much alive just after the release of *Phantasmagoria: A Puzzle of Flesh* when all evidence seemed to be pointing to the contrary (White). However, there is a caveat: usually people credit the resurrection of adventure games to corporations, but in fact, as I've shown, adventure game fans and their community-supported creativity in revisiting classic games have powered the resurgence.

With this type of success occurring outside their doors, the original studios have shown a new interest in their old properties. When LucasArts released the special edition of *The Secret of Monkey Island* in 2009, I visited the website for the release and found all the standard accompaniments to a new game: an opening flash animation, pictures of the swashbuckling pirate cast, widgets for every social network, a swordplay minigame (LucasArts). But the gameplay is familiar even as the visuals are fully transformed and the interface enhanced. The game is simultaneously classic and new, and the player can at any point switch back to "classic" view to witness firsthand the evolution from sprite graphics to high-resolution animated pirate worlds. The original was released in 1990, almost two decades prior to this remake. This is far more than the typical corporate repackaging of an old game with work-arounds to adapt it to new hardware: it more immediately resembles the efforts of the Anonymous Game Developers in fully reimagining and restoring the *King's Quest* games. And it is not the only remake to emerge: as I address later, new releases of several classics waited on the horizon, rebuilt for a changed interface.

It is not so surprising to see another remake among many: everywhere I look someone is retelling a familiar story. The box office is overflowing with remakes of classic, and not-so-classic, films—while it might not be as overrun as Florence with imitations of the great masters, the feeling of testing the waters by re-creating the familiar is everywhere. A successful young adult novel about wizards or vampires spawns legions of similar stories, and, inevitably, its own series of movies and video games. The gods of Greek mythology are being reborn on screen and on the page in Rick Riordan's *Percy Jackson* series. In the face of this constant cultural reinvention, why is one decades-old computer game so outstanding?

The release of the special edition of *Monkey Island* and its sequel could be dismissed in the same way we dismiss all these brands built from old stories: it is easy to sell an already loved story. This same reliance on tried-and-true brands makes a movie sequel a safer bet than an unknown property. The production cost of re-creating a game is also decidedly less than that of making a new game. There's no need to hire a team of writers when the dialogue and story are already written, and no need to hire particularly imaginative artists when they can simply rebuild what is already in front of them, however pixelated it might seem on a modern screen.

The Secret of Monkey Island special edition makes it playable on modern systems, while running the original game in current environments is much more of a challenge. While the current experience is aesthetically distinct from the original, in most ways it is a revitalization of the same story. However, there is another important point of evolution: *The Secret of Monkey Island* has been re-released for several platforms that didn't exist when the game was new—including the iPad.

ADVENTURE GAMES CROSSING PLATFORMS

While *The Secret of Monkey Island: Special Edition* made its way to touch interfaces in 2010, Telltale Games has ported several of its titles to the Wii and the iPad. As these moves indicate, though many of the re-releases and new productions coming out today resemble the classic games and evoke the ghosts of these abandoned sequels, others have been making attempts to modernize and adapt the adventure genre to new interfaces and environments, taking advantage of the comfortable coexistence of the genre with the interfaces that have given birth to new forms of causal games. Appropriately, these efforts were originally focused on the Nintendo platforms, as Nintendo DS and Wii both offer innovative spins on interaction that can give even point-and-click gameplay a different feel. Reinforcing the relationship between the avatar body and the player's body, the DS and Wii both make use of more immediate embodiment of actions. When playing the Wii, the player moves his or her entire arms, often imitating physically what the avatar does on the screen. When playing on the Nintendo DS, the player uses a stylus to interact directly with objects through a touch screen. Each platform reduces the barriers between player and avatar by eliminating one step of abstraction, the mouse. New series for these platforms have emerged with traditional adventure game play.

Zack and Wiki (2007), an adventure game for the Wii, makes use of the movement-responsive controller interface to enable users to solve puzzle-based levels. The narrative of Zack and Wiki is familiar: Zack is "a little pirate with big dreams" who "has his sights on being the greatest pirate that ever lived!" (Capcom)—just like Guybrush Threepwood in *Monkey Island*. Zack even has his own undead pirate to contend with, echoing the earlier game's themes. The multiplayer mode of *Zack and Wiki* imitates the experience of classic adventure games—many players gathered around a computer screen, pointing at possible solutions and guiding the player with the mouse. Rather than creating lots of Zack avatars on the screen, the multiplayer mode lets each secondary player use his or her controller to point and highlight as a crowd argues out possible solutions. This type of play taps into the casual games mimetic market: mimetic interfaces are those where the player's actions physically "mimic" what is accomplished on-screen, and thus include a level of physicality not traditionally associated with game interfaces. The spectacle of four players arguing over solutions to a puzzle and gesturing wildly with Wii remotes can add dimensions to the gameplay that go beyond the derivative narrative at the game's core.

For instance, plate 13 shows the hand-shaped cursors of three players indicating the path they want the main player to take in controlling Zack. The outlines and arrows follow the movement of the player's controllers as if the Wii remote were a marker for a digital whiteboard, while the main player directly manipulates Zack. While *Zack and Wiki* can only accommodate four players, other current projects make use of the potential of massive multiplayer gaming, thus taking the genre in yet another new direction.

The rise of mimetic interfaces extends the adaptability of game interface design across genres. While an arcade system used tailored input through buttons and joysticks, optimized entirely for the game hardwired in the system, consoles and PCs struggled to meet the needs of many different users. The interface of most console devices derived from the integration of the familiar joysticks and button pads into relatively standardized forms that each game could customize for its control set. PCs briefly had a number of popular interface peripherals such as joysticks but ultimately have been defined by reliance on the mouse and keyboard. The integration of motion responsiveness is replacing the touchpad and joystick on consoles, bringing with it the new point and click exemplified in *Zack and Wiki* and other Wii adventure games.

Meanwhile, game interfaces were also evolving to allow for a wide range of game experiences on mobile devices. The need to fit both display and interface into one device becomes more and more challenging with the demand for multifunction devices that occurred with the spread of mobile devices like smartphones and then tablets. Portable gaming platforms began to improve with the introduction of small touch screens, as in the Nintendo DS, which used a hybrid form of dual screens and keypads to accommodate adventure game titles such as the *Professor Layton* (2007–2012, Nintendo DS) and *Ace Attorney* (2001–2012, Game Boy Advance, Nintendo DS, iOS) series alongside real-time strategy and action games. But while the DS used the touch screen merely to augment existing interfaces, the touch screen began to overwhelm and replace the buttons for user input as new mobile devices got smaller and allowed even more multitasking in their intended functions. The *Professor Layton* games use the bottom, touchable screen for the exploration interface of the game, and the top screen for additional information or context during the puzzle.

Much of the interaction on touch screen–only input devices is accomplished with virtualization: as the screen can represent or respond to input anywhere, it can mimic a keyboard or cellphone number pad as the situation requires. By extension, the range of interfaces is seemingly limited only to the size of the display, although much of the tactile feedback that allows for quick interactions is lost as each virtual "button" has the same glossy smooth surface as any other section of the display. However, this capacity for transformation and mimicry has made touch screen devices the ultimate in convergent platforms, especially for the consumption of media.

KICKSTARTER AND ADVENTURE GAMES REBORN

As I've shown, Tim Schafer's Kickstarter success has both accompanied and inspired a flurry of interest in revitalizing old games, and both companies and game designers are following his lead. In embracing the Kickstarter model, the corporate community is embracing the practices of the fans, remaking games, extending old stories, and finding the continued potential in the arcs they once abandoned. This path of influence is a reversal of the norm. The corporate world is being influenced in its production choices by the fan world. This is different from using market research, when producers track audience desires and then try to create the games people are looking for, a practice that casts a broad net rather than targeting a group with shared gaming values and can lead to hollow and generic releases. Here, the commercial market is being driven by a tiny group of niche fans who have not merely displayed their devotion to a particular type of game but have also revealed what is still left in those games that might be attractive to others.

Some of the other creators following in Schafer's footsteps reference him in their campaigns' opening videos, including *Leisure Suit Larry*'s Al Lowe. Whereas Schafer's goal was to create an original production, Lowe promised to resurrect the original *Leisure Suit Larry in the Land of the Lounge Lizards* (1987, DOS/Apple II) with all-new art and possibly updated humor, if not gameplay. The very first *Leisure Suit Larry* game remains playable online thanks to the efforts of an open-source project, Sarien .net. This organization, a classic adventure game restoration project, has created browser-playable versions of old adventure games with a twist. Multiple players can be in the browser game at the same time, interacting while still going through the single-player storyline at their own pace. The set-up can lead to absurdity, with many clones of Larry (or Sir Graham—*King's Quest* has also been preserved for play in this way) wandering the streets together with no real way to distinguish one player's avatar from another. The core games are not even updated versions of the classics, but they allow players to cooperate on play in new ways.

Obviously, the game is still graphically of its time (and the pixilated women are far from the pseudo-realistic 3-D fantasy depictions that would follow). The 2012 Kickstarter project promises to graphically update familiar locations such as Lefty's Bar, pictured in plate 14, presumably for a new generation of players but also for many returning fans. The project was fully funded by nearly 15,000 backers pledging more than the $500,000 goal—not the spectacular numbers as Tim Schafer's campaign, but enough to show the viability of the model for onlookers. The higher-level pledge rewards offer a picture of the backers, with rewards for donating $5,000 including a sold-out unique opportunity to be immortalized within the game's text through a nonplayer character with the backer's face: "Be the broke gambler wandering the streets of Lost Wages wearing nothing but a barrel!" among other opportunities to be immortalized in the game (Lowe, "Make Leisure Suit Larry Come Again!"). Some of the highest-level sponsors are shown as new characters sitting at the bar in plate 14, with dialogue chosen in part by the backing fan. These are appeals not only to nostalgia but to fans with a sense of ownership and investment in the original game, those who want to be part of its story in a lasting, visible role in the new edition—and are willing to make sizable donations for the opportunity.

Originally, the small production company Replay Games, known mostly for casual mobile games, announced this remake with the intent of funding the project through a venture capitalist. However, the deal fell through, according to Replay, in part because the investors said that "we like your company but we want nothing to do with Leisure Suit Larry since it will tarnish our good name" (Lowe, "Make Leisure Suit Larry Come Again!"). Al Lowe noted the creative freedom that this new, fan-funded venture would allow the team, with no need to soften the edge of the central quest of a man in a polyester suit trying to lose his virginity to suit what Lowe referred to as a "Walmart" sales requirement. A nod was also made to the freedom of the fans: when released on 27 June 2013, the game was available without digital-rights management. The game structure implicitly endorses the involvement of fan creators alongside professionals, with the original creator collaborating with those his work inspired.

This type of tension between industry and personal production is not unique to video games. Independent films are viewed differently, and show different production qualities and concerns, than a Hollywood blockbuster; likewise, self-published books released on Amazon and other digital distribution networks every day often address topics and concerns that mainstream publishing would not support. Studio-produced game industry titles flirt with narrative, but ultimately reflect different concerns, budgets, platforms, graphics capabilities, and markets than truly independent game titles. Interestingly, the *Double Fine Adventure* and *Leisure Suit Larry* Kickstarter campaigns took different approaches to reconciling the expectations of a studio with the indie budget and crowd-sourced model, with *Double Fine* planning on a three-person development team initially but extending the scope of the project with the funding windfall, while Replay Games planned on a slightly larger team to target PCs instead of iOS. The funds needed for each project reflected this difference in intended project scale.

COMMUNITY SUPPORTED GAMING

As long as spaces outside traditional models of production and distribution are seen as the playground of the amateur, with "real" creative work eventually rising out of crowd-sourced and self-published models to receive accolades within the industry's usual forums, even projects such as Tim Schafer's *Double Fine Adventure* can be viewed suspiciously—models that work once, perhaps even twice, but ultimately lack the longevity of support in the Wall Street investment or venture capital models. While Double Fine's project was only the highest-funded campaign in Kickstarter's history for a short time, the campaign was quickly followed by a number of other successful efforts to fund adventure games, including several by other classic developers who hadn't revisited the genre for over a decade. Jane Jensen, creator of the *Gabriel Knight* series, has likewise been involved with two projects funded through Kickstarter—first as a designer working with the team behind fan-game *The Silver Lining* to create an original title, and later with a push for funding her own studio as a subscription-based initiative.

Jensen's 2012 Kickstarter campaign, intended to fund the first year of her new studio, Pinkerton Road, notes her status as "master storyteller" and offers a model for "community supported gaming," with the imagery of the Kickstarter reward shirts evoking a shared farm with new adventure games as the promised crop (Jensen). The successfully funded campaign involved backers during the process, even inviting votes on which of three possible games should be the studio's first production. Backers who donate enough to be considered members of the studio (a modest $50) are promised video and art updates, copies of all the games, and alpha and beta test opportunities so they can see the games evolve throughout the year—a recurring refrain of all the projects, but well summed-up in the "community supported gaming" slogan (Jensen).

On similar lines, the *Cognition* Kickstarter campaign for a new adventure game by Phoenix Studios, the team behind *The Silver Lining*, offered backers the chance to take on the honorary roles of deputy and assistant directors, complete with the chance to be part of creative meetings throughout the game development. This model of investing financial resources in return for the chance to view and, to a limited extent, participate in the process and give feedback is derived from the same communal investment model that made *The Silver Lining* possible. Although all episodes of *The Silver Lining* were released as free downloads, the campaign also offered an opportunity for players who enjoyed that game to give back by investing in the team's first commercial project. The new game was successfully funded, though it requested and received much less ($35,000 raised, $25,000 requested) than campaigns by veteran commercial teams (Phoenix Online Studios). Given that limitation, in many ways the team is still as independent and technically "amateur" as before. However, *Cognition* has been successful: as of June 2013, three episodes have been released, and the game has received several adventure game awards. (It is also notable as one of the fastest development processes, keeping close to the release schedule backers were promised by comparison to the extra year *Leisure Suit Larry Reloaded* spent in development.) *Cognition* was released on Steam's digital distribution network as of 28 June 2013, as part of Steam's "Greenlight" community-based game nomination and voting system.

Another Kickstarter campaign less directly tied to the adventure game genre (but also opening with a nod to Tim Schafer) has experienced success on a similar scale: *Shadowrun Returns* (Kickstarter 2012, 2013). The original *Shadowrun* was a pen-and-paper role-playing game not unlike *Dungeons & Dragons*, similarly adapted to a few video games and other formats. The world has been out of creator Jordan Weisman's hands for many of those adaptations, and he only recently reacquired the rights and gathered some of the original team behind the world's cyberpunk meets high fantasy concept. The campaign focused on the involvement of those creators and a return to the narrative that was at the core of *Shadowrun's* adaptations, including several novels—"the result should be an overall narrative that is layered, textured, and satisfying" (Harebrained Schemes LLC). This promise comes paired with the release of a level editor bundled with the game. As Jordan Weisman noted in his Kickstarter video, the original format of *Shadowrun* allowed for players to tell their own stories within the world, and the level editor will allow for that cocreativity to be part of the game again, with a corresponding online community for sharing those levels. This model of a shared creative space is not new, as other role-playing games, including Baldur's Gate, have bundled level editors as a successful part of their game ecosystem, but it is a particularly appropriate step given the reliance of *Shadowrun Returns* on a community of backers who will likewise be some of the storytellers drawn into the creative space. Other opportunities for cocreation have been built into this and other Kickstarter projects, such as the ability for backers to vote on a city to add to the finished game. The feeling of shared ownership and investment was successful, and the campaign raised nearly $2 million (Harebrained Schemes LLC).

Interestingly, crowdsourcing is also being extended to interactive fiction. The same effort to use a Kickstarter campaign to enable a storyteller to move from producing free creative works to receiving community support was reflected in the successful funding of Andrew Plotkin's latest interactive fiction project, *Hadean Lands*, in 2010. With $31,336 pledged in response to a request for $8,000 (a goal met the first day), the campaign for *Hadean Lands* would seem to reflect a demand for interactive fiction that few outside of that community would have anticipated (Plotkin, "Hadean Lands"). However, Plotkin is also the proven author of many lauded works, including the aforementioned *Shade*. Thus his success could be driven not only by recognition of his artistry but also by the fans who have played his many free creations. In his campaign pitch, Plotkin noted: "Not too many people have tried to make money off IF [interactive fiction] since the 1980s ended. But now is the time. Text is more popular than ever—what do you think Twitter is made of? People are reading. People are carrying around book-readers. I can write a world-class narrative game, and I think people will pay for that. So let's give commercial IF a shot" ("Hadean Lands").

Plotkin's specific mention of platform, and the carrying around of "book-readers," points to a resurrection of reading as a digital act. The form-factor also offers an answer to "Why interactive fiction now?" If a text-based game can be an experience that fits into the same time and space that "just" reading might previously have filled, then playing at reading can seamlessly fit where a computer program might not have.

NOSTALGIA AND RETROGAMING

Is this nostalgia, or something bigger? Tim Schafer asks himself that very question in a documentary about *Double Fine Adventure*. Nostalgia in gaming is common: signs can range from the availability of *Pac Man* car-seat covers and mirror dangles, to live action costumed re-creations of games in the street, to the popularity of games re-released or preserved from past decades. Suominen notes that the very playing of, and thus preservation of, nostalgic games—what he refers to as "retrogaming"—is part of a memory system of gaming: "The Internet seems to be a kind of a central processing unit of the memory machine in today's retrogaming. In addition to recollection narration, the Internet also makes many other forms of nostalgia possible. A gamer's personal work and their consequent 'inside' position are central in this kind of action" (Suominen). Yet the very term "nostalgia" is laden with a backward-looking stigma, and ultimately nostalgia could have been satisfied by replaying *Day of the Tentacle* rather than funding new games on Kickstarter. The investment of resources into looking forward, while remaining conscious of the genre's past, characterizes the current stage of the adventure game genre reloaded.

In his second update video, Schafer speculated on what makes point-and-click adventure games compelling enough for the genre to be worth revisiting. Considering the motives of the fan-investors, he noted that he was almost afraid to offer concrete details about the coming game because "the first adventure game promised infinite possibility," and this return to the form holds similar allure (Schafer). Kickstarter games are exciting precisely because they are unfinished, and fans are invited not only to peek into a process but also to play a role on some level in making the games possible and even in determining what the final game looks like (this is most evident in Jane Jensen's model for community supported gaming). A fully detailed game, by contrast, does not invite fans into its making: it appears too fully formed without their input.

Ultimately, the Kickstarter projects described here embody a new stage for that cooperation, with sources of funding based on the passion of fans traded for insight and some voice in the production process while investing in its outcome. This same approach is working in other industries with projects such as the incredibly well funded Pebble e-watch, a smartphone-compatible app-based watch that raised over $10 million despite setting an initial goal of a comparatively modest $100,000. Pebble offered a model for manufacturing goods that require a critical mass in guaranteed sales to be worth the production costs. But with games in particular, the community supported gaming that Jane Jensen's new studio embodies suggests both a transparency of production and a freedom from the expectations of gatekeepers in the rest of the industry. This freedom can be particularly empowering for narrative projects that would be considered experimental or risky, or perhaps even too controversial, in the eyes of mainstream investors.

The impact of crowd-sourced funding on production is critical. However, the transformation in distribution is also helping to enable not only a direct line to fans and players but also the very relevance of this particular genre. As Andrew Plotkin said in asking for support for his new work, eReaders and mobile devices offer a space where a narrative form thought previously antiquated can abruptly be innovative. Many of the Kickstarter-funded adventure games and reboots mentioned so far are being designed for the iPad and other tablets. The *Leisure Suit Larry* remake is promised for both iPad and Android, while *Double Fine Adventure* was originally promised for iOS only, and Andrew Plotkin's work will only be available on mobile devices, except for a special version for Kickstarter backers that will also be available for desktop computers. Even the smaller-scale project *Cognition* is aiming for an iOS release. This is unsurprising given that a number of adventure games, including resurrected projects such as *The Secret of Monkey Island Special Edition*, are already finding new audiences through these platforms, on which the old point and click is being replaced by touchable worlds where the "infinite possibilities" Schafer imagines for the genre are perhaps coming out to play.

CHAPTER 8

The iPad and the eBook

"iPad is our most advanced technology in a magical and revolutionary device at an unbelievable price," said Steve Jobs, Apple's CEO. "iPad creates and defines an entirely new category of devices that will connect users with their apps and content in a much more intimate, intuitive and fun way than ever before." (Smith and Evans)

STEVE JOBS, FOUNDING CEO of Apple, announced the "magical" iPad at launch in January 2010. The device, a touch-driven tablet, is a somewhat familiar yet meaningfully new platform, one that has spawned a new hardware market. The tablet followed on the heels of the iPhone and iPod Touch, both touch-driven platforms that eliminated the user's need for a separate control system for interacting with a wide range of applications. The iPad offered a higher screen resolution but did not have a legacy of compatible applications to take advantage of both its screen size and its processing power, opening the door to new applications vetted by Apple's approval process. Developers looking to build native apps needed to make a heavy investment, as Apple's development environment required Mac hardware. Thus the iPad on launch day offered the allure of an unexploited and uncrowded marketplace not yet brimming with an incredible range of professional applications. The solo or independent designer with an Apple computer willing to spend $100 for a license was able to download the SDK and develop an application. This is a steeper barrier to entry than rival mobile platform Android, which requires no investment and allows for applications developed on any system. However, Apple's approval process offers reassurances to users buying apps from unknown or independent developers. While the graphical resolution of the iPad's screen did allow for 3-D graphics, most designers opted to use the screen's crisp delivery to produce 2-D graphics and animations that played with representational aesthetics in new ways, since these require fewer artists than a full 3-D title, by its nature, demands.

The iPad was transformational. Throughout this text, I have been noting the primary platforms associated with particular works, revealing the impact of transformations in hardware capabilities and operating systems on digital storytelling. At first, digital storytelling took advantage of the shift from print books to keyboard and monitor, and eventually the mouse. The invention of consoles shifted some games to platforms with very different interfaces, as the examples of *Zack and Wiki* and *Professor Layton* convey. As hardware has changed, its forms have pushed works into particular shapes. But perhaps no hardware evolution in this varied past will prove as important to interactive narrative as the introduction of the tablet, and with it the elimination of many hallmarks of the computer interface in favor of an immediacy of touch that rivals a reader's physical interaction with a print book.

On first impression, the iPad may look like an overgrown iPhone. But it arrived with very different marketing and intended purpose. The 3.5-inch display of the iPhone lends itself to mobile and hurried consumption, evoking the image of the *Angry Birds* player catching a few spare minutes to hurl birds at pigs between meetings and thus playing a major role in the rising popularity of casual games. In contrast, the iPad's 9.7-inch screen suggests a different type of device, portable like a laptop or netbook but without the focus on the production interface and keyboard. The lack of a physical keyboard suggests that the iPad, like the iPhone, is intended for media consumption and not necessarily production. But what media?

The positioning of the iPad to support a wide range of forms, from books to film to games and music and the many forms in between, has empowered the device and those modeled on it to increase the relevance of electronic literature in mainstream media experiences. While the current generation might offer only the first glimmer of the potential, the iPad displays some of the "magic" Jobs alluded to at launch. Book designer Craig Mod has called it the "universal container," suited to forms of fixed and flexible content layout that storytellers are only beginning to explore (Mod). I'm wary of overstating the "universality" of the touch screen, though it is certainly true that it is a chameleon of interfaces, capable of imitating the surface if not the physicality of a range of user interfaces while also allowing for direct manipulation of objects on the screen. Lori Emerson rightly cautions against taking the interface of technology (which she defines as the "intermediary layer between reader and writing") for granted—and assuming that any interface, whether the touch of the iPad screen or the turning of the pages of the book, is truly invisible. To do so ignores the significance of the platform (Emerson). At the same time, the interface of the iPad is difficult to grapple with precisely because of its intended self-camouflage: in most applications it fades into the background, and the user is only aware of it when it intrudes.

From its launch the iPad needed to establish both a market and set of expectations for this new interface and hardware profile. Early responses were polarized, as David Pogue broke down in his review, offering first the advice for techies: "The bottom line is that you can get a laptop for much less money—with a full keyboard, DVD drive, U.S.B. jacks, camera-card slot, camera, the works. Besides: if you've already got a laptop and a smartphone, who's going to carry around a third machine?" But in his review for "everyone else," Pogue commented: "For most people, manipulating these digital materials directly by touching them is a completely new experience—and a deeply satisfying one." The success of the platform commercially has since been clearly confirmed by sales, particularly as competitors have released a range of tablets using the Android operating system and other models with the same general interface and application marketplace. The iPad's launch sparked an extraordinary day of application sales. New users, perhaps determined to immediately see the capabilities of the new device, downloaded one million apps on the first day (Schroeder). However, Pogue overstated the "completely new" experience at work: many of the applications that attracted attention as part of the iPad revolution were in fact deeply rooted in the genres I've examined here. Reconsidering those same forms, from books and gamebooks to adventure games, reveals their influence and a continuing stream of fan-communal production powering the iPad "revolution."

THE E(VOLVING) BOOK

In size and scale, the iPad most immediately reminded users of a book. Larger than a typical eReader, the iPad mimicked not a single open page but a spread of pages. From a historical perspective, the evolution of eBooks followed the transformation of mobile platforms. The addition of new creative tools and the corresponding change in the publishing industry have both influenced and been shaped by this progression. Apps began as transformed books, literally. Project Gutenberg (1971–, online) and similar projects began with scanned texts, and eventually used crowd-sourcing to transcribe the texts to a native digital form. Proprietary eBook formats, with corresponding software, were particularly important in the early days to protect a traditional model of copyright even in the face of radically transformed distribution and perceptions of ownership, and similar digital-rights management is embedded into most of the major text-centric eReader platforms, particularly Amazon's Kindle (introduced 2007) and Barnes and Noble's Nook (introduced 2009). But these files consisted primarily of text, or possibly scanned images, often distributed as a single aggregate that can convert to the page scale demanded by any particular device, screen, or font size preference. This conventional formatting of text corresponds to original commercial eBook formats, which were usually PDFs to preserve formatting. Andrew Piper critiques this absence of physicality in the digital text in his study on reading in an electronic age: "Digital texts lack feeling. All that remains of the hand is a ghostly remnant of its having been there at the time of scanning, like the chance encounters with scanners' hands from Google Books, accidental traces of the birth of the digital record." The touch screen offers a physicality for that digital record, complicating any understanding of the form as alienated from its codex predecessor. This hand of the reader-creator could be said to be even more absent in works born in and designed for the digital medium—even as the touch interface makes the screen stand in for the lost materiality, and thus offers the potential for digital works to be more than an imitation of a physical book.

Portability and touch were already essential to the rising popularity of eBooks when the original Kindle form-factor was introduced in 2007.

PCs proved deficient as reading devices because their lack of portability, less than optimal screen sizes, and display backlights made reading a less than pleasant experience. This opened the door for (single-purpose) eReaders. Their advantage over the physical book was their seemingly endless storage capacity. The Amazon Kindle and other early eReaders focused on delivering a clean experience of black-and-white text content. The Kindle owed much of its initial success to a screen that relied not on backlighting but on a form of digital ink that increased readability. Amazon also offered an always-available (and free) wireless service that allowed users of the Kindle to download books anywhere. Kindle users did not need to plan ahead or sync with their computer or home wireless network before a trip, making the Kindle function both as portable library unrestricted by its physical memory and as the world's best-stocked portable bookstore. However, that same technology could not support color images while meeting Amazon's goal of keeping the price attractively low, making books that originally had a text-heavy format best suited for the Kindle.

But just as the "single purpose" of consoles has been threatened by increased demands and expectations on the part of users, eReaders have moved from single-purpose devices to multifaceted ones, requiring more than an imitation of paper alongside digital distribution methods and inconvenient keyboard. The interface was a fundamental problem in transitioning these early eReaders, one that the touch screen alone could solve elegantly while maintaining the close relationship between the reader and the spatial dimensions of a print book. With processors getting smaller and more powerful, and touch screens more responsive and high resolution in their displays, the market opened to a surge of convergent devices that have quickly become indispensable: as of a 2013 Pew Internet report, 56 percent of American adults own smart phones (Smith). Smartphone capabilities are best exemplified by Apple's iPhone, itself the heir of Apple's iPods and the gradual transformation of first music and eventually much of media to digital distribution as a primary means of consumption. Users of the iPhone and its compatriots quickly became used to the touch screen as convergent interface for phone calls, texting, social networking, reading, and play, all explored through the same tiny lens. These experiences paved the way for the iPad, and they suggested the ways the new device could transform the consumption of media. In the case of the eBook, the iPad would immediately restore some of the tactility of the book—while changing readers' expectations for electronic texts as more than a port of a physical product.

The transformation of eBooks by the iPad began unremarkably, as Apple took advantage of the colorless display of the Kindle when marketing the iPad. At launch, the iPad included a free copy of *Winnie the Pooh* (1926), complete with color pictures. The image of the clear reproduction was shown over and over in marketing, but this was the least significant step forward that the iPad afforded. Rather akin to the early addition of graphics in adventure games as illustration rather than active content, iPad *Pooh*'s images were static and could still translate readily back to print. Unlike the promising projects on the frontiers of electronic literature that I described earlier, *Winnie the Pooh* was still an eBook as "book," essentially a scan and subject to the same awkward metaphors of page-flipping and ordered text. It is delivered through the iBookstore and displayed on a virtual bookshelf that mimics a traditional wooden shelf of covers, an incongruous interface that evokes nostalgia even as the rest of the device moves forward. The inclusion of this type of content as one of the selling points of the iPad only offered fuel to those who scoffed that it was just a device for consuming content. The packaging and closed development model led some to compare the iPad with a toy rather than a serious technical platform.

So how did the iPad become so successful upon its launch and eventually in revolutionizing the reading experience? Perhaps in one of the most surprisingly successful launch-day applications: *Alice for the iPad* (2010, iOS), a repackaging of the Lewis Carroll's *Alice in Wonderland* (conveniently in the public domain) with only a few small changes. Unlike *Winnie the Pooh*, which was constrained by the traditional eReader model of Apple's iBookstore, *Alice for the iPad* used the full capabilities of an application, or app. An app on the iPad takes over the entire screen as an independent software installation, and thus can include any combination of interactivity without regard to the definition of a book or ePUB format constraints. Thus *Alice*, rather than simply reproducing the text, was fully illustrated with simple interactive elements. Atomic Antelope, a developer that understood that launch buyers would be desperate for signs of the touch screen's novelty as a media device, immediately offered the $9 version of Lewis Carroll's novel with playful touches: a pocket watch that tilts with the screen, a falling jar of marmalade, an expanding and retracting Alice, and other such simple moving parts that are placed alongside the text. The childlike elements seem to suit the story even as they encourage the reader to skip past the static pages to find more movable goodies. A "Drink Me" bottle floats over the text when Alice finds the table with a little bottle on it, responding to a shift in tilt of the iPad itself; a view out a window changes, sliding from side to side to reveal more of the landscape than the original illustrations would let the reader gaze upon.

With these basic enhancements to the familiar story of falling down the rabbit hole, the *Alice* application became a perfect start for the interactive book craze, and was even featured in an Apple ad campaign emphasizing the device's "magic." The mechanics of the *Alice* app would not surprise a child familiar with the most basic pop-up or activity books. However, the seamlessness of the experience would ultimately attract a new audience. The touch interface opened the door to a range of users outside the typical reach of a tech product, particularly as parents began sharing their devices with children. The applications that followed *Alice* down the rabbit hole have each taken steps further toward a truly convergent form of storytelling.

At first, developers simply imitated the features of the *Alice* app. The same strategy paid off for *The Little Mermaid and Other Stories* (2010, iOS) and *War of the Worlds* (2010, iOS)—both beautifully created apps with clickable, tiltable, and otherwise active moving parts on top of an otherwise static object. For instance, the *War of the Worlds* app allows users to shoot at humans even as the text describes the alien invasion. The flashy animation that sometimes obscures the pages of text could be said to distract from the story, but it in fact recalls the definition of "ergodic" literature by making the reader work for the next piece of content. Is shooting at humans an enhancement or a distraction? Nothing about the story responds or transforms in even the slightest manner in response to the user's engagement with these gimmicks. It is possible to read the full novel as originally written without interacting with any of these pieces. The same level of interactivity as early point-and-click adventure games is possible, but it is still disconnected from the narrative—though a reconnection would come quickly to the platform.

GAMEBOOKS AND INTERACTIVE FICTION REVISITED

To examine the consequences of this transformation from book to interactive book, it is helpful to turn to Hayles's concept of the "material metaphor"—the traffic between words and physical artifacts, with which she reminds us that "to change the physical form of the artifact is not merely to change the act of reading (although that too has consequences the importance of which we are only beginning to recognize) but profoundly to transform the metaphoric network structuring the relation of word to world" (Hayles, *Writing Machines* 22–23). The revolution ongoing in books as applications is driven in part by awareness of the new platform's potential and the intentional design of experiences for these affordances. Closer to the experiments of electronic literature than traditional print books, books as apps can be interactive experiences. Often they include touchable words, interactive elements, sound, video, animation, and nonlinear elements. The juxtaposition of these book apps with conventional (though also "born digital") eBooks creates new expectations for the latter. When the same picture book was available as static images on the iBookstore and as a full application elsewhere, there was clearly no reason for the store to be limited to traditional codexes. Gradual advances in the iBooks format, the addition of an iBooks author to the development tools, and the rise of new ePUB formats using HTML5 as their foundation have begun to change the bookstore itself. Guides to the new ePUB format incorporate instructions on creating video, audio, links, and other basic interactivity (Castro). The addition of HTML5 to the standard is particularly telling as it evokes the originals of the hypertext novel and other early electronic literature. While those early experiments in electronic literature are now "out of print," because they were distributed on CDs and written for operating systems incompatible with current ones, their legacy of nonlinear organization and layered stories responsive to the intention of the users is clearly evident in the most recent generations of interactive books on the iPad and beyond.

In the transitional place between apps that originated in books, films, and stories intentionally designed as apps stands one series that, like adventure games and interactive fiction, provided early models for such narratives. The *Choose Your Own Adventure* (2012, iOS) series is now on the iBookstore, a new tactic following the resurrection of the books for the purposes of reaching reluctant readers where they are. Other apps have taken on the gamebook model and added new layers and influence from other gaming genres. The *Choice of the Dragon* iPad app (2010), one of several *Choice* games, is reminiscent of the "Endless Tales" and other *Dungeons & Dragons* gamebooks. The player takes on the role of a dragon in a medieval fantasy setting and engages in humorous confrontations. The app embeds elements borrowed from these role-playing games, so, for example, a reader-player's choices "shape" his or her dragon's stats, or strengths, and limit the options as the stories progress. A typical choice in the story goes like this:

> "Don't eat me!" jabbers one of the goblins. "Eat Grubsh! He's got meat on him!"
>
> The goblin who spoke pushes forward one of the other goblins with the butt of his spear. The other goblin, presumably Grubsh, drops his spear as he shakes in front of you.
>
> How cute. What do you do?
>
> Scare them off
>
> Slaughter them all

Each choice has consequences for later decisions—for instance, slaughtering the goblins increases the dragon's brutality and vigilance. The choice also influences the continuing relationship with the goblin horde, who can become the player's minions. The underlying platform of the *Choice* games is also worth noting: like *Adventure Game Studio*, *Choice* games share a common tool, *ChoiceScript*. The tool is designed for authors with no background in code, and is at the foundation of a collection of hosted free and commercial games made with the system. This model of a shared platform driving a range of creativity will appear again and again in my examination of iPad literature. It contradicts the conventional view of the iPad as a highly closed and walled garden, for community-driven tools breach that wall and its expectations.

In some ways, these app-books are more easily playable than their paper predecessors, as hyperlinks have eliminated the need to flip pages back and forth. But the tactile experience of the work—what led Zuzana Husárová and Nick Montfort to call the genre "shuffle literature"—is lost in translation: "What makes the approach of shuffle literature distinctive in contrast to the conventional codex novel and in contrast to computer-generated literature, for instance, is its stress on the reader's manual shuffling and the unusual, tactile perception of the discourse and how it is rearranged" (Husárová and Montfort). The term "shuffle literature" also evokes the iPod, with its mixable playlists, although the digital shuffle is disembodied, the traversal outsourced and handled by the computer. Christopher Rickaby (writing as James T. Raydel) wrote a novel appropriately called *Shuffle* (2012, Kindle) in which pieces of the story are linked to different songs on an iPod, allowing the reader to choose the song/chapter that he or she proceeds to next (Raydel). The threads of the stories are bound together by more than coincidence, but the final "reading" varies dramatically with each pass through. While the book could conceivably have been represented in print, the eBook-only release seems more appropriate.

However innovative the format, the central concept of taking on the role of "you" in an outlandish adventure remains unchanged. To some extent, these books exemplify the direction that iBooks, at least, sees as a future for its eBooks. One addition to the *CYOA* model enabled by the new eBook format is the addition of story maps that display the potential of choices to lead either down a further branch of the story or to a sudden stop. This feature makes it easier than ever to "cheat" in the book, replacing old strategies of marking the pages of past choices to read ahead before deciding whether to follow the story through. The original print novels were practically eBooks when they were written in text, and converting them to digital while preserving the intention of the original interactive elements is not a difficult adaptation. However, the appearance of these books in the iBookstore instead of as separate apps demanding their own rules system is an important transformation. They're in the iBookstore in part because of Apple's new tool for building eBooks, *iBooks Author* (2012), which has extended the range of embedded multimedia content and supported a move away from plain text and scanned images. *iBooks Author* definitely pushes beyond the old PDF-like model of eBooks and gives authors a wider framework for building books—a clear legacy of the type of thinking that led to the *CYOA* books in the first place, which started to break readers out of their linear expectations as part of building engagement.

The *CYOA* books serve as a proof of concept for *iBooks Author*, though the development tools hold potential for elements beyond these predictable models. The limited knowledge of programming or mastery required to produce interactive books with *iBooks Author* is akin to the accessibility of production that *Adventure Game Studio* and other editors offered to fans of the adventure game genre: now an author does not require a production team to include a measure of interaction in his or her releases. Apple's authoring software can also be viewed as an attempt to consolidate control over books on the iPad by expanding the possibilities within the iBookstore and potentially eliminating some of the experimentation inherent in creating a separate app.

Appropriately, interactive fiction has also followed the path to the iPad, with the *Frotz* reader providing a tool for reading interactive fiction content on the device. Its emulator brings the text-parser model to the convergent platform, allowing those few who both enjoy highly puzzle-focused text games and are willing to struggle through typing verbs on an iPad keyboard to play text-based games. And as Andrew Plotkin's Kickstarter project attests, this might be only the beginning for interactive fiction tools generated with the touch device in mind, as his *Hadean Lands* will have a new interface that will offer a model for future development (Plotkin, "Hadean Lands"). Unlike the *CYOA* books, which are enabled through the new eBooks format, experiments like interactive fiction interpreters remain stand-alone applications not yet under the wings of Apple's iBookstore. However, the project is also a testament to the distinction of Kickstarter from a guaranteed system for preordering or investing: it was funded in December 2010 and was still in development as of June 2013.

Andrew Plotkin also brought Jason Shiga's *Meanwhile* (2012, iOS) to the iPad. *Meanwhile* is a sequential web of story paths all built on a foundational choice between chocolate and vanilla ice cream. While the printed book broke down the original paths into a shuffle-text of colored lines for the reader to follow between sections of pages, the app presents the entire narrative space and the web of intersections, scale, and complexity. The structure (as shown zoomed out in plate 15) recalls Scott McCloud's concept of the "infinite canvas," which he envisioned as the transformative power of digital comics liberated from the page when contrasted to the linear demands of the printed codex (McCloud 200). The hybridization of the infinite canvas with the choice-based model of the gamebook offers a different model for approaching interactivity in comics, which, as Jared Gardner notes, defies definitions of comics that rely on their previously established formal properties (193). While panels and paths between them are clearly present in plate 15, the use of space reflects the needs of the simultaneous multiplicity of narrative choices.

INTERACTIVE PICTURE BOOKS

Alongside these reinventions and convergences of familiar genres, a crowded market of both converted and original picture books for the iPad has created a new marketplace. Most of these appear to be well-intentioned conversions of old texts to digitally enhanced versions, though at times the result seems designed more to turn the device into an engaging portable entertainment system than to extend the experience of the original text. Perhaps most important, the new format increases the cross-generational appeal that was already inherent in the content. Children's books like these are some of the best-selling apps on the iPad, even though the form factor and price tag might suggest otherwise: the *Alice for iPad* app is priced at $9 and has sold over half a million copies, while Dr. Seuss adaptations tend to be priced at under $5. Several apps, particularly Dr. Seuss classics including *The Lorax* (1971 print,

2012 iOS) and *Oh, the Places You'll Go!* (1990 print, 2011 iOS), clearly have a crossover audience driven by nostalgia—one reviewer called the apps "your childhood nostalgia deals of the day"—and for many such readers the "read to me" option might be decorative rather than meaningfully interactive (Barribeau). Many of these interactive picture books include reinforcement for language skills: click on an object, hear the name, and the word appears or is highlighted. In comparison to *Alice*, the original "magical book" app, the transformation is primarily visual and auditory. The applications adapted from Dr. Seuss's work are more immediately recognizable, and most of the additions serve as mediators for a child experiencing it—a voice narrator provides the option of reading the whole story or a single word aloud, while visual indicators connect text to corresponding image. Many of these features mimic the actions or engagement of an adult acting with the child reader, and the technology replaces or augments that role. I examine two examples that stand out among a crowded marketplace of interactive picture books: *The Fantastic Flying Books of Mr. Morris Lessmore* (2011, film/iOS) and *Lola and Lucy's Big Adventure* (2012, iOS).

Stories told on the physical page have long explored the magic of books: they are portals, gateways, links between worlds, and holders of endless knowledge. Whenever popular wisdom says that reading is on the decline, the loss is immediately linked to declines in imagination and education. So even as more technologies are involved in teaching and stimulating creativity, the book itself has remained a cultural fetish object, its power explored in film, television, and now on the iPad in the app *The Fantastic Flying Books of Mr. Morris Lessmore*. Originally a short film, Moonbot's *The Fantastic Flying Books of Mr. Morris Lessmore* is now perhaps one of the most aesthetically engaging apps to be released to the iPad to date. It is a fairy tale about a man who lives his life by the book and finds himself the caretaker of a room filled with magical books, each desperate to share its story with him. In this world, the love affair with books goes both ways—the books return their readers' love. The style of the film, rather like its content, is perched between traditional and modern aesthetic techniques. The iPad adaptation similarly straddles these worlds, using the film's haunting images as illustrations that come to life at a touch but still flip like the pages of a picture book. Sections of the pages hold hidden interactivity, like the letters of an alphabet cereal waiting to be rearranged or the keys of a piano ready to be played.

Although the player takes a role in the story, it is not as a character. On each page, the player can inspire change. Fittingly, the story opens with a reader surrounded by books: "Morris Lessmore loved words. He loved stories. He loved books. His life was a book of his own writing, one orderly page after another. He would open it every morning and write of his joys and sorrows, of all that he knew and everything that he hoped for." Over the static image the occasional trace of a sweeping white arrow encourages the reader to retrace it, and in doing so trigger the winds of change that will blow Morris Lessmore from the comfort of his home and into his journey. When the reader has sufficiently triggered the wind, the page turn appears, and along with it new text: "But every story has its upsets." In this case, the upset is the reader, whose actions power the story forward, though if only on its linear, predetermined path.

Is there anything gained in this hybridity? The layering of forms is itself evocative: the film explores the portal of the book, while Moonbot's app and game structures frame the reader-player-watcher's relationship with the content. The app and film offer different experiences, yet the added aspects of the iPad app aren't about narrative but about play. Perhaps the app's most powerful achievement is to bring a genre that is usually ignored to the attention of more viewers. Short films are the category at the Oscars least known to those not lucky (or interested) enough to attend the film festivals that in many cases are their only forum. Given that situation, even the best short films receive much less exposure than full-length features. Normal theater distribution has no system for showing these films, and online outlets make them available but not necessarily visible. The iPad has the potential to bring them to the nonspecialist, and the change in format that Moonbot has experimented with makes them more than yet another story to watch passively through iTunes or Netflix. The same attention to aesthetics and affordances is clear in Moonbot's second project, *The Numberlys* (2012, iOS), a storytelling app about the birth of the alphabet in a world of numbers. As metafiction, this is particularly fascinating: the story of bringing letters, and the narrative voice, into the space of numbers—which is what programming itself reduces to on a fundamental level.

While *The Fantastic Flying Books of Mr. Morris Lessmore* is linked to traditions from film, other interactive picture books bear more explicit connections to adventure games. The Pinkerton Studios Kickstarter launched Jane Jensen's community supported gaming. The studio started production with an interactive picture book for the iPad called *Lola and Lucy's Big Adventure* (Jensen). Lola and Lucy, shown in plate 16 with paw prints indicating the areas on the screen where interactions are possible, are two family bulldogs who set out on a journey to find their place in life, and discover through their adventure that they belong at home with their family.

Why would a woman who identifies herself as a "master storyteller" start out her new studio with an interactive picture book? Perhaps because there are a lot more similarities than differences between these genres, and the same design principles come into play in the construction of playful narrative whether in book or game form. As the screenshot in plate 16 of one page's hotspots indicates, the contents are interactive, and the positioning of the child in relation to the text invites exploration, as any element on the screen can respond to the child's touch. Touching the paint set dips the dog's paw in paint, unlocking a paint-smeared paw print that appears wherever the user touches next. This feature recalls the way the avatar brings the player into an adventure game, as the user's finger is identified with the dog's touch on the screen. Other minigames and events throughout the book invite the player either to assist or identify with Lucy and Lola through herding sheep, catching dog treats, and following or guiding the journey cross-country.

Although the title *Lola and Lucy's Big Adventure* suggests that the child reader is along as an observer on the dogs' journey, the involvement of a professional game designer in creating a work in this genre promises more involvement than mere observation. Even the title echoes the rhetoric of the adventure game genre, and of course the project emerges as the first from a company devoted to reviving story-focused play (Jensen). This combination appropriately reconnects the interactive books that are popular now to their predecessors in the history of graphic adventure games, demonstrating their similarities in form and intent concretely. Not only are adventure games not dead, but they are finding second life as part of the textual experience that helped inspire their creation, in a space between books and games that is increasingly well populated with texts that demand child and adult alike to act simultaneously as reader and player, exploring a story using frameworks that are inherently convergent in their use of media and interactive components.

While these new projects draw heavily on established traditions within the adventure game genre to construct new platforms for storytelling, the ideas established in the heritage of the "gamebook" are changing. In these examples, there is an explicit and well-structured relationship between the reader's actions and the motion of the story, as play is exploratory and revealing. The reader might not be the protagonist of the story, as in the old *CYOA* model, but the new interactive books encourage the reader-player to define his or her relationship to the story's material and to push the story-as-game to respond to his or her area of interest. In some of these story spaces, the reader-player does not need to explore all the text or pursue every quest, offering him or her the opportunity to view the story as a swimming pool, with opportunities for diving deep or skimming the surface. This similarity to the conventions and expectations of the golden era of classic adventure games, along with the promise of touchable environments, opened the door to several game relaunches: *The 7th Guest* (1993 PC, 2010 iOS), *Simon the Sorcerer* (1995 PC, 2010 iOS), and many more.

While many games on the iPad are ports of existing titles, there are also signs of the genre's rebirth in the development of new content. Aside from the Kickstarter projects discussed earlier, mainstay producers such as Telltale Games have brought many of their new series to the iOS platform. There are also several converging genres. Hidden object games are a casual spin on the adventure game, based on exploration and story, often with an explicit mystery or quest theme. Unlike an adventure game, in which most of the found objects have a clear relationship to progressing in gameplay, a hidden object game often includes objects that exist for the sake of being found. The player looks directly into the game world without an avatar, and the relationship of player and character is fairly direct. In an iPad-based exemplar of the genre, *Midnight Mysteries: Salem Witch Trials* (2010, PC/Mac/iOS), the player has to collect inventory objects and solve puzzles while also hunting for "hidden" objects and pursuing a mystery posed by the ghost of

Nathaniel Hawthorne. The player's exploration adds to the journal, written in first person and describing the quest:

> The date that I found on the gravestone worked as the code for the lock.
> That was tricky. Nobody gives me a warm welcome at the gates. That's ok,
> I can live with that. As far as I can see, the village looks deserted. I hope
> I am wrong. I need to find somebody who can help me find the grave of
> Hawthorne.

However these hybridizations are categorized, they rely on the structures of adventure games for their primary storytelling. These early digital genres are part of the new spectrum of electronic literature on the iPad, and together these works form a vision of a posthypertextual future of strongly participatory literature.

Magical Books

> She sent him another poem . . . the answer came back much too
> quickly, and it was the same answer as always: "I do so envy your skill
> with words. Now, if you do not object, let us turn our attention to the
> inner workings of the Turing machine."
> She had made it as obvious as she dared, and the Duke still hadn't
> gotten the message. He must be a machine. (Stephenson 318)

WHEN NELL CONTINUES her journey into the Primer, she is held captive in a prison of logic. The Duke of Turing advises her through the challenge, continuing to explain the workings of the Turing machine even as she tries to determine if the duke is friend or captor—man or machine. She confirms her suspicions by sending the duke poetry, considering the inability to comprehend literature proof enough of the duke's mechanical heart. It is too tempting when considering the intervention of new technical platforms into literary spaces to see the platform's affordances as the heart of a transformation; however, it is precisely in the human networks enabled by the machine that literature is being re-formed. Throughout this chronicle of the evolution of digital narrative genres, the role of fans and reader-players turned creators is impossible to overstate.

To return to Henry Jenkins and his concept of participatory culture: the media of interactive storytelling demand participation. And, perhaps more essentially, these media enable full participation through accessible tools and models for generating interactive works. Thanks to *Adventure Game Studio, Inform 7*, and *ChoiceScript*, along with the *iBooks Author* toolkit and the many emerging tools for iPad app development, the prerequisite for sharing interactive stories within these genres is not programming knowledge but desire. This distinguishes contemporary interactive story production powerfully not only from early computer games but also from modern mainstream commercial titles, both of which require much more technical knowledge. This revolution follows the pattern of the rise of the amateur across other media platforms. YouTube enabled the amateur film producer to reach a wide audience, while the availability of powerful film-editing programs empowered the individual to create more complex work. Blogs gave voice to a range of authors and relied upon easy-to-update publishing platforms with low barriers to entry. Advances in interactive storytelling as a form were already in the hands of amateurs in communities like that surrounding *Adventure Game Studio*; now that model for participatory culture extends across genres.

When the "Art of Video Games" exhibit opened at the Smithsonian American Art Museum in March 2012, the curators selected games to show the history and development of the medium, including several adventure games. The process for developing the list began with the curator's list of 240 games, narrowed to a final 80 games with the help of votes from the public in a form of curatorial crowdsourcing, appropriate given the role fans have played in sustaining and supporting the history of games. This openness to public participation perhaps explains some of the repetition in the list (among eighty games, there are four of Nintendo's *Zelda* titles, one of the best-selling and most recognizable franchises still active today), but it also offers a portrait of a medium still in development. As exhibit curator Chris Melissinos notes in his preface to the exhibition book:

> It is precisely their interactivity that provides video games the potential to become a superior storytelling medium. I say potential because video games are still in adolescence. The advantage that books, movies, and television have over video games is with time only. Like all other forms of media, hindsight will tease inspired works from the digital past, and these will serve as the cornerstones of great works yet to be created. (Melissinos and O'Rourke 8)

This process of building new ways of storytelling on the foundations set by classic games is already under way. However, it is happening outside the mainstream game industry, in the fringes where the definition of game doesn't always seem to apply, in the spaces in between media where convergent storytelling allows for playful reading and reading as strategy of play. And another layer of interactivity surrounds the development of innovative ways of telling stories that is even more essential: the interactions of storytellers and readers, of programmers and creators, of fans turned world-builders.

It is precisely the interactivity among a range of users surrounding these new platforms that offers the potential for this convergence to more radically shape the future of eBooks. Like Nell with her Primer, a generation is growing up with a convergence of reading and play in their earliest experience. The marketing of these convergent forms is currently skewed toward the young. The term "digital natives," coined by Marc Prensky, is often used to refer to young people's comfort with multitasking with digital technologies that the older generation in theory does not use so readily. The term evokes the image of a child as master of online environments, and to some extent familiarity does bring a level of mastery, but many fear that the generation raised on digital technologies will be less likely to appreciate storytelling (Prensky).

When we talk about literature in a digital world, it's often with an undercurrent of fear: will today's multitasking youth even appreciate canonical literature? The short answer is yes, as continued sales and markets for Young Adult literature in particular reflect, but nonetheless the relationship of readers with stories is changing. In "reading" her Primer, Nell is at play, just as the child with his or her iPad or the player of a text-based game participating in the writing of the story through his or her typed actions are. Convergent devices are the natural home for convergent literary forms, with adventure games existing alongside electronic literature and traditional texts. For the children being raised now on the adventure game–inspired interactive picture books, will there be a recognizable line between reading and playing? That line is already fading. And as these games incorporate coloring books and easy to manipulate elements, will creating be another part of the same experience?

The wider transformation of our platforms, production, and distribution models alongside convergence of forms and genres will inevitably alter our perception of storytelling and our relationship with text.

Perhaps the true "digital native" will be judged by his or her ability to create and tell stories within communal spaces. Bolter noted that the participatory act of the reader of electronic work demands a new type of authorship: "The writer must practice a kind of second-order writing, creating coherent lines for the reader to discover without closing off the possibilities prematurely or arbitrarily. This writing of the second order will be the special contribution of the electronic medium to the history of literature" (*Writing Space* 144). I'll close with a few examples from the iPad that point to that "special contribution," drawn from a communal construction of genres that bridge the space between book and game until such binaries are rendered unnecessary.

ELECTRONIC LITERATURE ON THE IPAD

Given the range of the permutations of eBooks, it has become difficult to isolate the domain of electronic literature. Florian Cramer challenges us to think about the relationship between print and eBooks this way:

> If we take the word literature literally, as everything written with letters, then electronic literature today is no longer the exception but the norm. Paper publishing has largely become a form of Digital Rights Management for delivering PDF files in a file sharing-resistant format (but also, a more stable form of long-term storage of digital content than electronic storage). In the age of smartphones, tablets and e-readers, reading has largely shifted towards electronic media if we consider all writing that an average person reads per day. Is this the electronic literature we mean?

My answer to this provocation must be simultaneously yes and no. It is impossible to talk about electronic literature without noting this more common experience of reading on screens, and the convergence of eBook forms with interactive works means that forms once outside of the mainstream are becoming more visible. I examine the current state of electronic literature on the iPad through two exemplary works: Dave Morris's *Frankenstein* (interactive novel, 2012) and Erik Loyer's *Strange*

Rain (electronic literature, 2010). Each represents one direction of experimentation on the iPad, from co-opting existing worlds to produce playable fanfiction, to the adaptation of prior print projects to a medium better suited to their possibilities, to the use of new affordances to re-create the fundamental structures for "reading."

Aesthetic innovation alongside new interfaces for the novel can transform interactions, as in the *Frankenstein* app by Dave Morris. Mary Shelley's story is one of the earliest science fiction novels, and it is familiar enough that even the nonreader often "knows" the story thanks to film adaptations, plays, and even Mel Brooks's movie and musical. Adding an iPad application borrowing from the approach of the *CYOA* series to this plethora of adaptations doesn't involve superseding the original text as much as complementing it, encouraging the reader to reengage with the familiar story. Dave Morris created *Frankenstein* with *inklewriter*, a free platform for making a next-generation form of shuffle fiction. The most powerful pieces of the *Frankenstein* app put the reader closer to the perspective of the "creature," allowing the reader to decide what is interesting and how to deal with life in close proximity to humans. While the story's progression is still faithful to the world of the original narrative, the app allows the player enough choices to make it an exploration of humanity. It is only appropriate for a text that considers the possibility of the "ghost in the machine" to explore the moral dimensions of knowledge through the creature's eyes.

Of course, the *Frankenstein* app is still primarily text derived from and built around the original story structure, but the experience of the creature's agency, and at times lack thereof because of the reactions of characters in the story, provides a framework within which readers can play with both social expectations and individual responsibility in relationship to the text's primary themes. Part Two begins with the player sharing the creature's perspective upon awakening:

> This is not the warm wet that you knew all that time in the tank. It rattles off the ground, sluices your body—cold, dark, uncomforting. In your hand a soft thing, snatched from a hook. You wrap it around you, shivering.
>
> Everything at once. It's too much. These are separate sensations that need to be sorted so that the world makes sense.

Do you concentrate on what you can see?
Or on your hearing?
Or on developing your coordination?

The choices grow more complex, as when the creature learns about the history of humanity and is asked to "judge which side is dominant," good or evil. The creature's understanding or resentment of humans grows as he reads John Milton's *Paradise Lost*, fragments from the Greek historian Plutarch, and notes from Thomas Jefferson's travels—even as his reading of Frankenstein's diary pushes the creature toward despair and self-awareness. The literalness of the old *CYOA* books, with their second-person address (what do "you" do?) was at times heavy-handed. The same decision-making model in the *Frankenstein* app is striking and meaningful. It's not just about "you" as character—it's "you" as the reader, directing your attention to different elements within the story.

The *inklewriter* platform also recalls *AGS* in its construction. Anyone can easily build and share interactive content with it following the rules of the system. The same platform powers a follow-up app, *Future Voices* (2012, iOS), which features stories chosen through an open competition: "The competition was a roaring success, with a glut of entries, some late-night shortlisting. The finished app contains 11 stories by writers from all around the world, and of all ages. There's a wide-ranging mix, from beautifully written pieces with very light interactivity, to puzzles, adventure games, madcap comedy, ethical dilemmas and ghost stories" (inklewriter). This versatility, combined with the collaborative, communal model appropriated from fan communities, reveals the potential for broader consumption and authorship of this type of interactive storytelling.

While the *inklewriter* apps play with publishing models and put new twists on familiar forms, other electronic literature is exploring the significance of the touch interface. Nowhere is this play with boundaries more explicit than in the highly layered narrative of the experimental app *Strange Rain*, one of the most recent and experimental apps in the iPad collection. The app is structured on two levels, as a kinetic rain simulator with an embedded narrative. *Strange Rain* probes not only the reader's expectations of interface but also the motion of storytelling, using the continual downpour of rain as a metaphor for a narrative where only some droplets can be experienced at a time while a picture of the larger storm emerges from these fragments. It is an experience that defies description—creator Erik Loyer described it as "a portable rainy day" (Gross). And the app has evolved since its initial release, incorporating a "feed" mode that replaces the story with tweets pulled from a Twitter search but displayed outside the context of the Twitter account, a stripping of context that Mark Sample describes "as if the tweet were the player's own thoughts, making the feed mode more intimate than you might expect" ("Strange Rain").

The vision of *Strange Rain* has abandoned the metaphor of pages altogether. The app encourages you to indulge in holding it over your head and watching the rain "fall" on you, and the rain itself is responsive to your actions. But in the "story" mode, the app acts just as responsive to gesture, and your motion conveys your interest in pursuing the character's line of thought. Unlike the Twitter mode, the story mode offers a coherent—if fragmented—narrative written by Erik Loyer. The fragments are thoughts from a man faced with a family crisis.

The story emerges in fragments triggered by each touch:

"I can think out here." "Insurance stuff seems to be going as smooth as can be expected." "The moment just before impact; I can't imagine how horrific it must have felt." "She'll pull out of it OK." "I hate thinking of her alone in that room." "Finally, some peace and quiet." "The walk from the parking lot is the worst." "It's easier to shove certain thoughts aside when we're away from the hospital."

In that sense, it's the most adaptive text yet on the iPad: what you move and touch actually changes what you see, instead of just triggering a quick reaction. Mark Sample has observed that the "poetics of motion" of *Strange Rain* move forward yet also are interrupted by touch: "The text is precipitously and perilously fragile and inadvertently escapable. The immersive nature of new media that years ago Janet Murray highlighted as an essential element of the form is entirely an illusion" ("Strange Rain"). The affordances of the iPad itself provide the mode of interaction and can also break from the story, closing the app. It's hard to imagine the model being successful for a novel, since it doesn't allow for the processing of much text in one sitting, but for text as experience—in which the point of entry is less important than the feeling of being in the middle of it—it's the most future-forward app to date, owing a great debt to the traditions of electronic literature and pointing toward an experimental future.

There are several other experiments worth noting in current electronic literature on the iPad. Many involve minimal narrative but create meaning through juxtaposition of ideas: Jody Zellen's *4 Square* (2012, iOS) recalls the location-based social network "Foursquare," but ultimately works as a combinatory toy, allowing for the rearranging of texts and images on a four-square grid to create evocative meaning. Similarly, Robert Hudecek's *Careless Observations* (2011, iOS) begins with the text "You do not need to wear your shoes all the time, but you should always know where they are" and offers an evolving photo journal-travelogue, complete with reader submissions. Other iPad experiments draw on poetics of motion, such as Jason Edward Lewis's *The Great Migration* (2011, iOS). Lewis labels the work a "P.o.E.M.M," or "Poem for Excitable (Mobile) Media," and showcases moving text arranged as "beasties" who spill their words only when touched.

NEW WORLDS TO CONQUER

"So as you can see, Princess Nell, the Land Beyond is not really a Turing machine at all. It's actually a person—a few people, to be precise. Now it's all yours."

King Coyote led Princess Nell back into the heart of his keep and . . . showed her the books containing the rules for programming Wizard 0.2, and other books explaining how to make atoms build themselves into machines, buildings, and whole worlds.

"You see, Princess Nell, you have conquered this world today, and now that you have conquered it, you'll find it a rather boring place. Now it's your responsibility to make new worlds for other people to explore and conquer." King Coyote waved his hand out the window into the vast, empty white space where once had stood the Land Beyond. "There's plenty of empty space out there." (Stephenson 405)

Nell's adventures through the Primer bring her first through a deeper understanding of machines and their rules, and finally face to face with the storytellers who together have built the world. But her adventure does not end as a consumer of the content of others: now that she understands the systems that built the world around her, she can create her own spaces. King Coyote (an alias for the Primer's main programmer) offers the tantalizing challenge to colonize the "empty space" waiting within the digital world around them. Ultimately, this is the invitation the interactive story makes to its readers: to explore it, conquer it, build upon it, and move beyond its boundaries. Fundamentally, the human-fan-collaborative level is where change is happening. Interactivity occurs beyond and through a work, enabled by convergent narrative. Immersion exists beyond a single text: the platform of the iPad is as significant to immersion as any one app. The works of current interactive storytelling defy any expectation of completion or finality, completely in opposition to what Walter Ong described as some of the defining characteristics of print and print narrative.

The convergence inherent to these new forms of storytelling will have an effect far beyond these texts, reaching to the definition of literature. Under its names including interactive fiction and adventure games, electronic literature is too important to the construction of people's relationships with texts to be viewed separately from the codex, particularly as the publishing industry and authors experiment with convergent forms both as part of marketing and as a way to fundamentally redefine a text. These convergent forms thus far, and the revived adventure game and its intersecting forms, have overcome obstacles thanks to innovations in production, distribution, and interface. The adventure game's history suggests that users' involvement in the transformation of these works, from rebuilding *Mystery House* to extending Don Woods's *Colossal Cave Adventure*, will always be part of the process of production. The community-driven creativity behind the *Adventure Game Studio* and similar production is not going anywhere. It is only growing, as the many Kickstarter project successes reflect. This community involvement in production, whether officially through level editors and moddable games or unofficially through fan remakes and sequels, is becoming more acceptable to the companies that hold the copyright to the content. And the emphasis that these works place on the personal appeal—on Tim Schafer's convincing desire to return to his beloved genre, on Al Lowe's convincing passion for the long-stagnant world of *Leisure Suit Larry*—reunites even these scaled-up productions with the values of the communities of fans that fund them. This approach is already moving some of the rights to forgotten projects back into the hands of design teams supported by dedicated groups of fans rather than a hope for widespread commercial success.

Digital distribution's power cannot be overstated, as it gives the successful app developer, game creator, or electronic storyteller the same means to reach an audience as any publishing house, without the need for approval by a gatekeeper. At its best, online distribution opens the door to people typically marginalized within creative communities and can lead to a greater diversity of stories than a survey of mainstream computer gaming would now reveal. The ability of women designers such as Jane Jensen to attract support through Kickstarter, rather than the more controlling influence of a venture capitalist, promises even further evolution of post–*King's Quest* women avatars. As small projects and motivated individuals or small teams continue to find funding and distribution through digital platforms, the range of creative voices present in convergent spaces will only grow, a key part of extending the storytelling space beyond familiar genres and the well-trodden patterns of heroic quests.

As these new voices find their platforms, convergent devices will allow for continual evolution of the structures available to storytellers. The boundaries between interfaces have always hindered convergence in the past, as the divergence in genres and forms of interactivity designed for consoles and PCs already demonstrated. Now, though, new interfaces are gradually bringing the separate gaming platforms back toward the same trajectory. The touch screen is an essential first step to convergent interface affordances, though there are others around the horizon—the Kinect and other touch- and gesture-responsive interfaces suggest the projection of stories within immersive environments. Furthermore, the linked genres of augmented and alternate reality games promise story spaces that invade reality, with collaborative models for storytelling across platforms already emerging that extend interactivity and erase any pretense of finality in authorship.

As these platforms continue to evolve, new forms will push outside the boundaries of our current spectrum. Just as the Kinect offers a model of indirect interface that was once the stuff of science fiction, so too are adaptive texts such as Nell's Primer within reach. Narratives have only begun to take advantage of the database potential of electronic literature, and certainly worlds with the complexity of the novels of James Joyce or even J. R. R. Tolkien lend themselves to more nuanced adaptations and inspiration than the current generation of interactive literature would suggest. The *Frankenstein* app, with a storyteller extending a world beyond the boundaries the original author explored, and similar forays into electronic literature offer a good glimpse of what is to come. Ultimately, the *Frankenstein* app is itself a work of fan production that also serves simultaneously as literature and critique. As copyright holders continue to move toward recognizing and cooperating with fan producers, particularly within the genre of interactive fiction, the possibilities for the meaningful construction of layered narratives will only grow. Consider the potential for a storytelling world on a fully interactive space, evolving through collaboration in the manner of Reality-on-the-Norm or the shared storytelling of multi-user dungeons: is such a vision really that far beyond what these adventure games in convergence are already gesturing toward?

These tangled threads of interactive storytelling offer a glimpse of the future of "literature," a word fraught with as many tensions and as much baggage as "art," but already partially claimed by the aspirations of electronic litterateurs. Reader-player-creators, fans turned creators who both build and use new tools for interactive storytelling, will navigate the possibilities of electronic literature by establishing models for a future in which the tools and affordances of each medium of storytelling is integrated seamlessly on convergent devices that offer a cacophony of narratives from both professional and amateur storytellers. With Nell, the readers of interactive stories will become the creators, building (new worlds) through communal tools for others to conquer and explore.

Aarseth, Espen. *Cybertext: Perspectives on Ergodic Literature*. Baltimore: Johns Hopkins University Press, 1997.

———. "Playing Research: Methodological Approaches to Game Analysis." *Digital Arts & Culture Conference*. Melbourne, 2003. http://hypertext.rmit .edu.au/dac/papers/Aarseth.pdf.

Adams, Douglas, and Steve Meretzky. *The Hitchhiker's Guide to the Galaxy*. Infocom, 1984.

AGDI. "King's Quest III Redux FAQ." February 2011. *AGD Interactive*. http:// www.agdinteractive.com/games/kq3/faq/faq1.html.

AGS. "Adventure Game Studio FAQ." n.d. http://www.adventuregamestudio. co.uk.

———. *AGS Forum Statistics*. 7 January 2009. http://www.bigbluecup.com /yabb/.

Aihoshi, Richard. "Myst Online Interview." 26 February 2007. *RPG Vault*. http://rpgvault.ign.com/articles/767/767789p3.html.

Akril. *Adventure: The Inside Job—Extras*. 2008. http://akril15.com/games/atij /behindthescenes.html.

Akril15. "Adventure: The Inside Job." 28 October 2008. *Adventure Game Studio Forum*. http://www.bigbluecup.com/yabb/index.php?topic=35962.0.

———. "Adventure: The Inside Job." 2008. *Quisquilious: Akril's Webpage*. http://akril15.com/games/atij/atij.html.

Alexander, Bryan. *The New Digital Storytelling: Creating Narratives with New Media*. Santa Barbara, Calif.: Praeger, 2011.

Anonymous Game Developers. "The History of King's Quest II." 2010. *King's Quest II: Romancing the Stones*. http://www.agdinteractive.com.

———. "Remake Release Information." 2010. *King's Quest II: Romancing the Stones*. http://www.agdinteractive.com.

Anthony, Piers. *Demons Don't Dream*. New York: Tor Books, 1993.

Anthropy, Anna. *Rise of the Videogame Zinesters: How Freaks, Normals, Amateurs, Artists, Dreamers, Drop-outs, Queers, Housewives, and People Like You Are Taking Back an Art Form*. New York: Seven Stories Press, 2012.

Atomic Antelope. *Alice for the iPad*. 3 April 2010. https://itunes.apple.com/us /app/alice-for-the-ipad/id354537426?mt=8.

Barribeau, Tim. "Dr. Seuss and Where's Waldo Are Your Childhood Nostalgia

Deals of the Day." 2 March 2012. *Everything iCafe*. http://www.everything
icafe.com/dr-seuss-and-wheres-waldo-are-your-childhood-nostalgia-deals-of
-the-day/2012/03/02/.

Barthes, Roland. *Image-Music-Text*. London: Fontana, 1977.

Barwood, Hal, and Noah Falstein. *Indiana Jones and the Fate of Atlantis*.
LucasArts, 1992.

Bellatti, Andy. "Interview with Roberta Williams." 25 October 1999. *Adventure
Classic Gaming*. Online.

Bethesda. *Elder Scrolls: Arena*. Bethesda Softworks, 1994.

Blank, Trevor. "Toward a Conceptual Framework for the Study of the Internet."
In *Folklore and the Internet: Vernacular Expression in a Digital World*, ed.
Blank Trevor, 1–20. Logan: Utah State University Press, 2009.

Bogost, Ian. *How to Do Things with Videogames*. Minneapolis: University of
Minnesota Press, 2011.

Bollier, David. *Viral Spiral: How the Commoners Built a Digital Republic of Their
Own*. New York: New Press, 2008.

Bolter, Jay David. *Writing Space: Computers, Hypertext, and the Remediation of
Print*. Mahwah, N.J.: Lawrence Erlbaum Associates, 2001.

Bolter, Jay David, and Richard Grusin. *Remediation: Understanding New Media*.
Cambridge, Mass.: MIT Press, 1999.

Borland, John, and Brad King. *Dungeons and Dreamers: The Rise of Computer
Game Culture*. Emeryville, Calif.: McGraw-Hill, 2003.

Bronner, Simon. "Digitizing and Virtualizing Folklore." In *Folklore and the
Internet: Vernacular Expression in a Digital World*, ed. Trevor Blank, 21–66.
Logan: Utah State University Press, 2009.

Cadre, Adam. *9:05*. 2000. http://adamcadre.ac/if.html.

Capcom. *Zack and Wiki: Quest for Barbaros' Treasure*. Capcom, 2007.

Castro, Elizabeth. *EPUB: Straight to the Point—Creating ebooks for the Apple iPad
and Other ereaders*. Berkeley, Calif.: Peachpit Press, 2011.

Chaplin, Heather, and Aaron Ruby. *Smartbomb*. Chapel Hill, N.C.: Algonquin
Books, 2005.

Chooseco, LLC. *Choose Your Own Adventure: About Us*. 2012. http://www.cyoa
.com/pages/about-us.

Cowlishaw, Tim, Rufus Pollock, Tom Chance, Matt Lee, Adnan Hadzi, Cory
Doctorow, et al. "Open Letter from Free Culture UK." June 2006. http://
www.bbc.co.uk/creativearchive/news/archives/2006/06/open_letter_fro
.shtml.

Cramer, Florian. "Post-Digital Writing." *Electronic Book Review*, 12 December
2012. http://www.electronicbookreview.com/thread/electropoetics/postal.

Crawford, Chris. *Chris Crawford on Interactive Storytelling*. Berkeley, Calif.: New
Riders Games, 2004.

Crowther, Will. *Colossal Cave Adventure*. 1976.

Cyan. "Myst." Broderbund, 1993.

Disney. *Toy Story Read-Along*. 1 April 2010. https://itunes.apple.com/us/app
/toy-story-read-along/id364376920?mt=8.

Doctorow, Cory. *Content*. San Francisco: Tachyon, 2008.

Dulin, Ron. "Phantasmagoria: A Puzzle of Flesh Review." 10 December 1996.
Gamespot. http://www.gamespot.com/.

Edison Interactive. *Night of the Meteor*. 18 October 2012. http://www.night-of
-the-meteor.de/index.php.

Ellison, Harlan, David Mullich, and David Sears. *I Have No Mouth and I Must
Scream*. Cyberdreams, 1995.

Emerson, Lori. "Activist Media Poetics: Electronic Literature against the
Interface-Free." Modern Language Association National Convention, Seattle.
http://loriemerson.net/2012/01/12/activist-media-poetics-electronic-liter
ature-against-the-interface-free-mla-2012/.

Fox, David. *Zak McKracken and the Alien Mindbenders*. Lucasfilm Games, 1988.

Fritz, Ben. "Variety Eliminates Chief Film Critic Position." 8 March 2010. *Los
Angeles Times*. http://latimesblogs.latimes.com/.

Gardner, Jared. *Projections: Comics and the History of Twenty-First Century Storytelling*. Stanford, Calif.: Stanford University Press, 2012.

Gee, James Paul. *What Video Games Have to Teach Us About Learning and Literacy*. New York: Palgrave Macmillan, 2003.

Gilbert, Ron. *Maniac Mansion*. Lucasfilm Games, 1987.

———. *Monkey Island 2: LeChuck's Revenge*. LucasArts, 1992.

———. *The Secret of Monkey Island*. Lucasfilm Games, 1990.

———. *The Secret of Monkey Island: Special Edition*. LucasArts, 2009.

Glorious Trainwrecks. *Glorious Trainwrecks*. n.d. http://www.glorioustrain
wrecks.com/.

Gould, Amanda Starling. "A Bibliographic Overview of Electronic Literature."
20 April 2012. *Electronic Literature Organization*.

Grodal, Torben. "Stories for the Eye, Ear and Muscles: Video Games, Media,
and Embodied Experiences." In *The Video Game Theory Reader*, ed. Mark J.
P. Wolf and Bernard Perron, 129–155. New York: Routledge, 2003.

Gross, Doug. "The Stormy Intrigue of Hit App 'Strange Rain.'" 24 January
2011. *CNN Tech*. http://articles.cnn.com/2011-01-24/tech/strange
.rain_1_entertainment-app-iphone-ipad?_s=PM:TECH.

Grossman, Dave. *Tales of Monkey Island*. Telltale Games, 2009.

Grossman, Dave, and Tim Schafer. *Day of the Tentacle*. LucasArts, 1993.

Guaraldi, Ben. *Star Trek: A Myth for Our Time*. n.d. http://www.bluesock.org
/~ben/writinghtml/024.html.

Gygax, Gary, and David D. Sutherland III. *Advanced Dungeons & Dragons: Dungeon Master's Guide*. TSR, 1979.

Harebrained Schemes LLC. "Shadowrun Returns." 29 April 2012. *Kickstarter*.

http://www.kickstarter.com/projects/1613260297/shadowrun-returns
/posts.

Hayles, N. Katherine. "Electronic Literature: What Is It?" 2 January 2007. *Electronic Literature Organization*.

———. *Writing Machines*. Cambridge, Mass.: Mediawork, 2002.

Hills, Matt. *Fan Cultures*. London: Routledge, 2002.

Hoelscher, Kevin. "I Have No Mouth and I Must Scream Review." 31 October 2002. *Adventure Gamers*. http://www.adventuregamers.com/articles/view
/17464.

Howe, Zack. "Review: Indiana Jones and the Infernal Machine." 20 March 2000. *Adventure Classic Gaming*. http://www.adventureclassicgaming.com
/index.php/site/reviews/148/.

Husáróva, Zuzana, and Nick Montfort. "Shuffle Literature and the Hand of Fate." *Electronic Book Review*, 5 August 2012. http://www.electronicbook
review.com/thread/electropoetics/shuffled.

IGN.com. *Best of 2006*. 2006. http://bestof.ign.com/2006/pc/2.html.

inklewriter. "Future Voices Competition." 27 January 2013. *inklewriter*. http://
www.inklestudios.com/inklewriter/future-voices-competition.

Jenkins, Henry. *Convergence Culture: Where Old and New Media Collide*. New York: New York University Press, 2006.

———. *Fans, Bloggers, and Gamers: Media Consumers in a Digital Age*. New York: New York University Press, 2006.

———. "Game Design as Narrative Architecture." In *First Person: New Media as Story, Performance and Game*, ed. Noah Wardrip-Fruin and Pat Harrigan, 118–120. Cambridge, Mass.: MIT Press, 2002.

———. *Textual Poachers: Television Fans & Participatory Culture*. New York: Routledge, 1992.

Jensen, Jane. "Jane Jensen's Moebius and Pinkerton Road Studio." 14 May 2012. *Kickstarter*. http://www.kickstarter.com/projects/1005365109/jane
-jensens-pinkerton-road-2012–2013-csg.

Jensen, Jane, and Roberta Williams. *Gabriel Knight*. Sierra On-line, 1990.

Juul, Jesper. *A Casual Revolution: Reinventing Video Games and Their Players*. Cambridge, Mass.: MIT Press, 2010.

———. "Games Telling Stories?" July 2001. *Game Studies* 1.1. http://www.game
studies.org/0101/juul-gts/.

———. *Half-Real: Video Games between Real Rules and Fictional Worlds*. Cambridge, Mass.: MIT Press, 2005.

Kirby, Carrie. "Avatars, Attorneys in a New World of Virtual Law." 27 April 2009. *SF Gate*. http://www.sfgate.com/business/article/Avatars-attorneys-in
-new-world-of-virtual-law-3163046.php.

Klink, Flourish. *Muggle Studies*. 2012.

Kücklich, Julian. "Precarious Playbour: Modders and the Digital Games

Industry." 2005. *Fibreculture Journal*. http://www.journal.fibreculture.org /issue5/kucklich.html.

LaFarge, Paul. "Why the Book's Future Never Happened." 4 October 2011. *Salon*. http://www.salon.com/2011/10/04/return_of_hypertext/.

Landon, Brooks. "Less Is More: Much Less Is Much More: The Insistent Allure of Nanotechnology Narratives in Science Fiction." In *NanoCulture: Implications of the New Technoscience*, ed. N. Katherine Hayles, 131–146. Chicago: University of Chicago Press, 2004.

Landow, George. *Hypertext 2.0: The Convergence of Contemporary Critical Theory and Technology*. Baltimore: Johns Hopkins University Press, 1997.

LaVigne, Chris. "Out of Order." 10 March 2004. *Pop Matters*. http://popmatters .com/multimedia/reviews/o/out-of-order.shtml.

Lessig, Lawrence. *Free Culture*. New York: Penguin, 2004.

———. *Remix: Making Art and Commerce Thrive in the Hybrid Economy*. New York: Penguin, 2008.

Leung, Jonathan. *Video Game Maps*. 2012. http://www.vgmaps.com/Atlas/PC /King'sQuest-QuestForTheCrown-Daventry.png.

Levinson, Paul. *New New Media*. Boston: Penguin Academics, 2009.

Lindner, Michael J. *Companions of Xanth*. Legends Entertainment, 1993.

Linkola, Joonas. "Sam and Max Hit the Road." 5 March 2004. *Adventure Gamers*. http://www.adventuregamers.com/article/id,78.

Lowe, Al. *Leisure Suit Larry in the Land of the Lounge Lizards*. Sierra On-Line, 1987.

———. "Make Leisure Suit Larry Come Again!" 2 May 2012. *Kickstarter*. http:// www.kickstarter.com/projects/leisuresuitlarry/ make-leisure-suit-larry-come-again.

Lowood, Henry, Devin Monnens, Andrew Armstrong, Judd Ruggill, Ken McAllister, Zach Vowell, and Rachel Donahue. *Before It's Too Late: A Digital Game Preservation White Paper*. International Game Developers Association, 2009.

Loyer, Erik. *Strange Rain*. 8 November 2010. https://itunes.apple.com/us/app /strange-rain/id400446789.

LucasArts. *The Secret of Monkey Island*. 2010. http://www.lucasarts.com.

LucasFan. *Another One Bites the Dust*. n.d. http://www.lucasfangames.de/.

MacCormack, Andrew. "A Tale of Two Kingdoms." 12 November 2007. *Adventure Gamers*. http://www.adventuregamers.com/article/id,819/p,2.

Manguel, Alberto. *A History of Reading*. New York: Viking, 1996.

Manos, Dimitris. "Interview with Rebecca Clements of Cirque de Zale." 18 August 2004. *Just Adventure: Inventory 14*. http://www.justadventure.com /Interviews/Rebeca_Clements/Rebeca.shtm.

Matos, Xav de. "Silver Lining Devs Want to Purchase King's Quest License from Activision." 27 March 2010. *Joystiq*. http://www.joystiq.com/2010/03/27/sil ver-lining-devs-want-to-purchase-kings-quest-license-from-ac/.

McCloud, Scott. *Reinventing Comics: How Imagination and Technology Are Revolutionizing an Art Form*. New York: William Morrow, 2000.

McGonigal, Jane. *Reality Is Broken*. New York: Penguin, 2011.

McLuhan, Marshall. *Culture Is Our Business*. New York: Ballantine Books, 1970.

———. *Understanding Media: The Extensions of Man*. 1964. Reprint, Cambridge, Mass.: MIT Press, 1994.

Meadows, Mark Stephen. *Pause & Effect: The Art of Interactive Narrative*. Indianapolis: New Riders, 2003.

Melissinos, Chris, and Patrick O'Rourke. *The Art of Video Games: From Pac-Man to Mass Effect*. New York: Welcome Books, 2012.

Meretzky, S. Eric. *Zork: The Forces of Krill*. New York: Tor, 1983.

Mills, Craig. *King's Quest 1: The Floating Castle*. Berkeley, Calif., 1995.

Mod, Craig. "Books in the Age of the iPad." March 2010. @*craigmod*. http://craigmod.com/journal/ipad_and_books/.

Montfort, Nick. "Mystery House Taken Over." 26 March 2004. *Turbulence*. http://www.turbulence.org/Works/mystery/.

———. *Twisty Little Passages: An Approach to Interactive Fiction*. Boston: MIT Press, 2005.

Montfort, Nick, and Ian Bogost. *Racing the Beam: The Atari Video Computer System*. Cambridge, Mass.: MIT Press, 2009.

Montgomery, R. A. *House of Danger*. Waitsfield, Vt.: Chooseco, 1982.

Moonbot Studios. *The Fantastic Flying Books of Mr. Morris Lessmore*. July 2011. https://itunes.apple.com/us/app/fantastic-flying-books-mr./id438052647?mt=8.

Morganti, Emily. "King's Quest IV: The Perils of Rosella." 29 September 2006. *AdventureGamers*. http://www.adventuregamers.com/article/id,682/.

Morr, Kenyon. *King's Quest 2: Kingdom of Sorrow*. Berkeley, Calif., 1996.

———. *King's Quest 3: See No Weevil*. Berkeley, Calif., 1996.

Morris, Sue. "WADS, Bots and Mods: Multiplayer FPS Games as Co-creative Media." 19 October 2003. *Digital Games Research Association*. http://www.digra.org/dl/db/05150.21522.pdf.

Moulthrop, Stuart. "For Thee: A Response to Alice Bell." *Electronic Book Review* (2011): Secondary Threads: Fictions Present. Online.

———. "Preface." In Michael Joyce, *Disappearance*. New York: Steerage, 2012.

Murray, Janet H. *Hamlet on the Holodeck: The Future of Narrative in Cyberspace*. Boston: MIT Press, 1998.

O'Dwyer, Arthur. "Colossal Cave: The Board Game." 20 April 2012. *Kickstarter*. http://www.kickstarter.com/projects/765522088/colossal-cave-the-board-game.

Ogles, Jacob. "Maniacs Make a Modern Mansion." 23 December 2004. *Wired* 12.8 (2008). http://www.wired.com/gaming/gamingreviews/news/2004/12/66109.

Ong, Walter J. *Orality and Literacy.* London: Routledge, 1982.

Pearce, Celia, and Artemesia. *Communities of Play: Emergent Cultures in Multiplayer Games and Virtual Worlds.* Cambridge, Mass.: MIT Press, 2009.

Perron, Bernard. "From Gamers to Players and Gameplayers." In *The Video Game Theory Reader,* ed. Mark J. P. Wolf and Bernard Perron, 237–258. New York: Routledge, 2003.

Phillips, Terry. *Advanced Dungeons & Dragons Adventure Gamebook 4: The Soulforge.* TSR, 1985.

Phoenix Online Studios. "Cognition: An Erica Reed Thriller." 11 December 2011. *Kickstarter.* http://www.kickstarter.com/projects/postudios/cognition-an-erica-reed-thriller.

Phoenix Studios. *Open Letter from The Silver Lining Team.* 28 February 2010. http://www.tsl-game.com/.

Pierce, David. "The Legion of the Condemned: Why American Silent Films Perished." *Film History* 9.1 (1997): 5–22.

Pinsky, Robert, Steve Hales, and William Mataga. *Mindwheel.* Synapse Software, 1984.

Piper, Andrew. *Book Was There: Reading in Electronic Times.* Chicago: University of Chicago Press, 2012.

Plotkin, Andrew. "Hadean Lands: Interactive Fiction for the iPhone." 6 December 2010. *Kickstarter.* http://www.kickstarter.com/projects/zarf/hadean-lands-interactive-fiction-for-the-iphone.

———. *Shade.* 2000. http://eblong.com/zarf/if.html.

Pogue, David. "Looking at the iPad from Two Angles." *New York Times,* 31 March 2010. http://www.nytimes.com/2010/04/01/technology/personaltech/01pogue.html?pagewanted=2&_r=0&hp.

Poole, Steven. *Trigger Happy: Videogames and the Entertainment Revolution.* New York: Arcade, 2000.

Prensky, Marc. "Digital Natives, Digital Immigrants." *On the Horizon* 9.5 (2001).

Pumaman. "Abandonware." 2 January 2004. *Adventure Game Studio Forums.* http://www.bigbluecup.com/.

Ratliff, Marshall, and Philip Jong. "The Rise and Fall of Full Throttle." 26 August 2008. *Adventure Classic Gaming.* 28 January 2010. http://www.adventureclassicgaming.com/.

Raydel, James T. *Shuffle: An E-novel.* Newcastle, U.K.: Tonto Books, 2012.

Reality-on-the-Norm. *Reality-on-the-Norm.* 2008. http://ron.the-underdogs.info/.

Rehak, Bob. "Playing at Being: Psychoanalysis and the Avatar." In *The Video Game Theory Reader,* ed. Mark J. P. Wolf and Bernard Perron, 103–127. New York: Routledge, 2003.

Rettberg, Jill Walker. "Electronic Literature Seen from a Distance: The Beginnings of a Field." *dichtung-digital* 2012. http://www.dichtung-digital.org /2012/41/walker-rettberg.htm.

Roper, Bill. "PC Graveyard: Warcraft Adventures." n.d. *Gamespot*. http://www .gamespot.com/.

Ryan, Marie-Laure. "The Interactive Onion: Layers of User Participation in Digital Narrative Texts." In *New Narratives: Stories and Storytelling in the Digital Age*, ed. Ruth Page and Bronwen Thomas, 35–62. Lincoln: University of Nebraska Press, 2011.

Saighman, Jim. "Uru: Ages Beyond Myst." 4 February 2002. *Adventure Gamers*. http://www.adventuregamers.com/article/id,347/p,2.

Salen, Katie, and Eric Zimmerman. *Rules of Play: Game Design Fundamentals*. Cambridge, Mass.: MIT Press, 2004.

Sample, Mark. "Strange Rain and the Poetics of Motion and Touch." 5 February 2012. *Sample Reality*. Modern Language Association National Convention, Seattle. http://www.samplereality.com/2012/02/05/strange-rain-and-the -poetics-of-motion-and-touch/.

Scavenger. "Kickstarter for New Tim Schafer Adventure Game Project." 9 February 2012. *AGS Forums*.

Schafer, Tim. "Double Fine Adventure Campaign." 13 March 2012. *Kickstarter*.

———. *Full Throttle*. LucasArts, 1995.

Schafer, Tim, Peter Tsacle, and Eric Ingerson. "Grim Fandango Puzzle Document." *Game Design Document*. LucasArts, 30 April 1996.

Schneider, Jan. "Interview with Ken Williams." 5 December 2003. *Adventure-Treff*. http://www.adventure-treff.de/artikel/interviews/ken_williams_e.php.

Schroeder, Stan. "iPad Stats: More Than 300,000 Sold on First Day, 1 Million Apps Downloaded." 5 April 2010. *Mashable*. http://mashable.com/2010/04 /05/ipad-stats-300000-sold/.

Schuessler, Jennifer. "The Muses of Insert, Delete and Execute." *New York Times*, 26 December 2011.

Shiga, Jason. *Meanwhile*. New York: Amulet Books, 2012.

———. *Meanwhile*. 13 May 2011. http://itunes.apple.com/us/app/meanwhile /id373198654.

Short, Emily. *Mystery House Possessed*. Mystery House Taken Over Collection, 2005.

Sierra On-Line. *King's Quest IV Advertisement*. 1988. http://www.adventure gamers.com/screenshot.php?id=6035&article=682.

Silver Lining. *The Silver Lining Game*. n.d. http://www.tsl-game.com/.

SkyGoblin (Markus). *Adventure Game Studio—Now Open Source*. 8 July 2011. http://www.skygoblin.com/2011/adventure-game-studio-now-open-source -again/.

Sluganski, Randy. "Sam N Max 2: The Most Important Game of the 2004 E3."

2004. *Just Adventure.* http://www.justadventure.com/articles/SamnMax2/SamnMax2.shtm.

Smith, Aaron. *Smartphone Ownership 2013.* New York: Pew Internet, 2013. http://pewinternet.org/Reports/2013/Smartphone-Ownership-2013/Findings.aspx.

Smith, Colin, and Bill Evans. "Apple Launches iPad." 27 January 2010. *Apple Press Info.* http://www.apple.com/pr/library/2010/01/27Apple-Launches-iPad.html.

Snarky. "Forum Rules." 15 April 2012. *AGS Forums.* http://www.adventuregamestudio.co.uk/forums/index.php?topic=45786.0.

Sowa, Tom. "Cyan Makes It Official: Myst Now in the Hands of Its Fans." 12 December 2008. *Spokesman Review.* http://www.spokesmanreview.com/.

Spear, Peter. *The King's Quest Companion.* 3rd ed. Berkeley, Calif.: Osborne McGraw-Hill, 1993.

Stephenson, Neal. *The Diamond Age: Or, a Young Lady's Illustrated Primer.* New York: Bantam Books, 1995.

Suominen, J. "The Past as the Future? Nostalgia and Retrogaming in Digital Culture." 2007. *Fibreculture Journal* 11. http://journal.fibreculture.org/.

Telltale Games. *FAQ.* 2009. http://www.telltalegames.com/monkeyisland/.

Thomas, Bronwen. "'Update Soon!' Harry Potter Fanfiction and Narrative as a Participatory Process." In *New Narratives: Stories and Storytelling in the Digital Age,* ed. Ruth Page and Bronwen Thomas, 205–219. Lincoln: University of Nebraska Press, 2011.

Totilo, Stephen. "The Sequel They Had No Right to Make—Now Has a Surprise Twist." 3 May 2010. *Kotaku.* http://kotaku.com/5529809/the-sequel-they-had-no-right-to-make-now-has-a-surprise-twist.

Twelve, Vince. *WLBSWHEAC Postmortem.* 26 November 2006. http://xiigames.com/2006/11/29/wlbswheac-post-mortem-part-one-concept/.

Wardrip-Fruin, Noah. "Playable Media and Textual Instruments." In *The Aesthetics of Net Literature: Writing, Reading and Playing in Programmable Media,* ed. Peter Gendolla and Jörgen Schäfer, 211–388. Bielefeld, Germany: Transcript, 2007.

Webster, Emma Campbell. *Lost in Austen: Create Your Own Jane Austen Adventure.* New York: Riverhead Trade, 2007.

Weis, Margaret, and Tracy Hickman. *The Annotated Chronicles.* Renton, Wash.: Wizards of the Coast, 1999.

Wells, Audrey. *Look What They've Done to My Game, Ma! King's Quest Gets a Facelift.* n.d. http://www.agdinteractive.com/pub-01.php.

White, Craig. "Interview with Roberta Williams." 1998. *Just Adventure.* http://beta1.justadventure.com/Interviews/Roberta_Williams/Roberta_Williams_Interview_1.shtm.

WikiNews. "Interview with BBC Creative Archive Project Leader." 22 June 2006. *WikiNews*. http://en.wikinews.org/wiki/Interview_with_BBC_Cre ative_Archive_project_leader.

Williams, Roberta. *King's Quest I: Quest for the Crown*. Sierra On-Line, 1984.

———. *King's Quest IV: The Perils of Rosella*. Sierra On-Line, 1988.

Williams, Roberta, and Ken Williams. *Mystery House*. On-Line Systems, 1980.

Young, Rosemary. "King's Quest: Mask of Eternity Review." December 1998. *Quandary*. http://www.quandaryland.com/jsp/dispArticle.jsp?index=237.